Using C on the UNIX System

Using C on the UNIX System

A Guide to System Programming

David A. Curry

O'Reilly & Associates, Inc.
103 Morris Street, Suite A
Sebastopol, CA 95472

Using C on the UNIX System
by David A. Curry

Copyright © 1985, 1987, 1988 Purdue Research Foundation.
Additional material copyright © 1990 O'Reilly & Associates, Inc. All rights reserved.
Printed in the United States of America.

Editor: Tim O'Reilly

Printing History:

January 1989:	First edition by David A. Curry.
March 1989:	Second printing. Minor revisions.
November 1989:	Third printing. Minor revisions.
March 1990:	Fourth printing. Minor revisions.
February 1991:	Fifth printing. Minor revisions.

This book is printed on acid-free paper with 50% recycled content, 10-15% post-consumer waste. O'Reilly & Associates is committed to using paper with the highest recycled content available consistent with high quality.

ISBN: 0-937175-23-4   [3/92]

Table Of Contents

Examples

Preface

Documentation Conventions
Acknowledgements

This book is intended for the person who wants to become a systems programmer for the UNIX operating system. Nearly all of the system calls and library routines provided by the operating system are discussed, and numerous examples of "real world" applications have been provided. The main focus of the discussion is on the 4.2BSD and 4.3BSD releases of UNIX from the University of California at Berkeley. Where serious differences exist however, both the Berkeley and AT&T System V environments are described.

The chapters have been organized in a "bottom up" fashion, presenting first the methods and routines for performing simple tasks, and then moving on to complex operations that build on the earlier information.

Chapter 1, *Introduction*, presents some introductory concepts and terminology. It also briefly describes the error handling mechanism used by the routines in the standard I/O library.

Chapter 2, *The Standard I/O Library*, and Chapter 3, *Low Level I/O*, present the high- and low-level input and output mechanisms provided for the programmer.

Methods of manipulating ordinary files and directories are described in Chapter 4, *Files and Directories*, and operations on special device files are presented in Chapter 5, *Special Files*.

Chapter 6, *Information About Users*, describes how to obtain information about the users of the system.

Chapter 7, *Telling Time and Timing Things*, describes the method for obtaining the time of day, as well as how to time various events.

Chapter 8, *Processing Signals*, describes both the Berkeley and System V signal and interrupt mechanism.

Chapter 9, *Executing Programs*, describes methods for executing other programs, including setting up pipes, and Chapter 10, *Job Control*, describes job control mechanisms for controlling those programs.

Chapter 11, *Interprocess Communication*, describes both Berkeley sockets and the System V shared memory, message queues, and semaphore mechanisms.

Chapter 12, *Networking*, describes the mechanisms for intermachine communication using TCP/IP.

Chapter 13, *The File System*, provides information on the internal organization of the UNIX file system.

Chapter 14, *Miscellaneous Routines*, covers a variety of miscellaneous shorter topics, including reading and setting resource limits, access to environment variables, and the use of *perror* for error handling.

The appendices provide information on some specialized topics that are not often used by the systems programmer, but are nevertheless good to know. Appendix A presents information on how to call FORTRAN subroutines from a C program, and vice-versa. Appendix B describes the use of Berkeley UNIX pseudo-terminals. The method for reading data structures from operating system memory is presented in Appendix C. Appendices D and E provide implementations of the Berkeley UNIX directory routines and an interval timer version of a "nap" function which sleeps for sixtieths of a second.

A modest background is required to understand the material in this book. The reader is expected to be fluent in the C programming language including the more advanced concepts such as structures and pointers. Good familiarity with the organization and use of the UNIX operating system is also a must. Although not necessary, familiarity with data structures and algorithms such as those used for sorting and searching will be useful.

The examples in the book are nearly all complete, working programs that should be entered and experimented with to gain a complete understanding of the material.*

Documentation Conventions

For the most part the conventions followed in this book should be obvious, but for the sake of clarity, we'll review them here. This handbook uses *italics*, constant-width and *constant-italic* text to emphasize special words:

Italics   are used for the names of all UNIX utilities, directories and filenames, and to emphasize new terms and concepts when they are first introduced.

Constant Width   is used for system calls, library routines, sample code fragments and examples. A reference in explanatory text to a word or item used in an example or code fragment is also shown in constant width font.

Constant Italics   are used in code fragments to represent general terms that require context-dependent substitution. For example, in describing the syntax of a system call, *args* means that a call would take some appropriate arguments. Obviously, since all variable names are arbitrary, the use of courier italic instead of courier is a fine distinction. We use it only when we think it will make things clearer.

function(n)   is a reference to a man page in section *n* of the *UNIX Programmer's Manual*. For example, *tty*(4) refers to a page called *tty* in Section 4.

---

*If you have internet access, or are a UUNET subscriber, you need not type in the examples. As a UUNET subscriber, you can copy them to your system with the following command:

```
uucp uunet!~uucp/nutshell/usingC/example.shar.Z /usr/spool/uucppublic
```

If you are on the internet, login to uunet.uu.net with anonymous ftp. Then type the following commands:

```
cd /nutshell/usingC
binary
get example.shar.Z
```

The file is a compressed shell archive. To restore the files once you have retrieved the archive, type:

```
uncompress example.shar
sh example.shar
```

For more information on UUNET, see the Nutshell Handbooks *Managing UUCP and Usenet* and *Using UUCP and Usenet*.

Acknowledgements

An early draft of this book was originally prepared while I was a systems programmer at Purdue, and was in fact first "published" by Purdue for use on campus in 1985. It was significantly revised and expanded in 1987 for 4.2 and 4.3 BSD, at which point I brought it to the attention of Tim O'Reilly. It was then further revised and adapted for publication as a Nutshell Handbook.

I am grateful to Clem Cole, Kent De La Croix, Jeff Schwab, and Dave Taylor for taking the time to read the book and make comments and suggestions. Without their help, several parts of this manuscript would have been a real mess. I would also like to thank Debbie Huffman of the Purdue Research Foundation for wading through the paperwork to get this book published. I'd also like to thank Kate Gibson, Daniel Gilly, Tom Scanlon, Sue Willing and Donna Woonteiler, of the production staff at O'Reilly & Associates, who made all the last minute edits to the book, created the index, and did all the other things necessary to make a manuscript into a finished book. Finally, I am especially grateful to Tim O'Reilly, who was willing to take a chance with me.

1

Introduction

System Calls vs. Library Routines
Versions of UNIX
Error Handling

Over the past several years, the use of the UNIX operating system has become widespread as workstations and personal computers that use UNIX have become cheaper and more powerful. Several books have been published on the use of UNIX, and on the use of the C programming language, which is the primary language used with UNIX. However, very little has been written about programming in C specifically for the UNIX operating system.

As a result, those wanting to write systems programs under UNIX have had to learn the hard way, by perusing the often inadequate documentation provided with the operating system, and by examining the source code of existing utilities. Although that is a good way to discover some of the more intricate and clever ways of doing things, it really isn't a satisfactory way to get started.

This book is an attempt to remedy that situation. It discusses in detail the use of most of the system calls and library routines available to the C programmer on the UNIX operating system.

It is not intended to be an introduction to C programming, nor can it really be considered an "advanced C programming guide." Rather, it has been written for the person interested in learning to become a "systems programmer" for the

UNIX operating system. The student who wishes to work for a university computer center, a systems programmer unfamiliar with UNIX who must now write programs for a UNIX PC or workstation, a bulletin board operator using a UNIX system to support his operation, and the researcher interested in writing his own tools to perform his work will find the material presented in this book useful.

The reader is expected to be fluent in C programming, including the more advanced concepts such as structures and pointers. The ideal reader will have been programming in C for at least six months, and will have had at least a minimal introduction to data structures and computer algorithms such as those used for sorting and searching. A junior (or perhaps a sophomore) in a college-level computer sciences curriculum should have no trouble with the concepts presented here.

Throughout this book small, heavily commented examples have been provided to demonstrate how the various routines being discussed are actually used. You will benefit by actually typing these examples in, compiling them, executing them, and then experimenting with them in order to observe first-hand how they operate.

System Calls vs. Library Routines

Before discussing the library routines and system calls provided by the UNIX system, a few preliminaries must be gotten out of the way. First, the difference between a system call and a library routine needs to be explained. These terms are often used incorrectly, even by those people who should know better.

A *system call* is just what its name implies—a request for the operating system to do something on behalf of the user's program. For example, `read` is a system call which asks the operating system to fill a buffer with data stored on a disk drive (or other device). Since great chaos would result if everyone were able to access devices whenever they pleased, this service must be requested of the operating system, which (often transparently) keeps track of all requests dealing with each device.

A *library routine*, on the other hand, does not usually need the operating system to perform its work. An example of a library routine is the `sin` function, which computes the sine of an angle expressed in radians. Since this is done simply by summing a finite series, the operating system is not needed.

In order to avoid confusion, when the difference is unimportant, this book will use the word *routine* to describe either a system call or a library routine.

Versions of UNIX

The main focus of the book is on the 4.2BSD and 4.3BSD releases of UNIX from the University of California at Berkeley.* Although System V is usually taken to be the "standard" UNIX, there are several reasons for discussing the Berkeley environment. Some of these are:

- Most university and government computer centers that use UNIX use Berkeley UNIX, rather than System V. There are several reasons for this, but perhaps the two most significant are that Berkeley UNIX provides networking capabilities that until recently (Release 3.0) were completely unavailable in System V, and that Berkeley UNIX is much more suited to a research environment, which requires a faster file system, better virtual memory handling, and a larger variety of programming languages.

- Sun Microsystems, with the largest installed base of UNIX workstations, uses a Berkeley-based operating system. Although it is true that Sun has been moving toward System V compatibility, their operating system is still much more like Berkeley UNIX than anything else. Other vendors, such as IBM, also provide releases of Berkeley UNIX for their university workstation customers.

- Older UNIX variants, such as Version 7 from Bell Laboratories and early versions of Xenix and Venix, are much closer to the Berkeley programming environment than the System V environment. Most of the material presented in this book, unless it refers to Berkeley-specific items, applies equally well to these older systems. Much of the material presented in books on System V will not.

Of course, System V is also quite widely used. For this reason, in the areas where System V differs greatly from Berkeley UNIX, both environments are discussed. This is especially true in Chapter 5, *Device I/O Control*, and in Chapter 11, *Interprocess Communication*. In these chapters, complete descriptions of both the Berkeley and System V environments, with examples, are provided.

---

*The 4.3BSD release is virtually identical to 4.2BSD as far as the material discussed in this book is concerned. For the sake of simplicity, we will use the term "Berkeley UNIX," rather than the official, but more cumbersome "Berkeley Software Distribution, 4.*x*," when the difference is unimportant. When we need to be specific, we will refer to these releases as 4.2BSD and 4.3BSD, respectively. Generally, any new functionality introduced in 4.2BSD remains the same in 4.3BSD.

Error Handling

A few words must be said about error handling. All of the routines in the Standard I/O Library (see Chapter 2, *The Standard I/O Library*) return one of the predefined constants EOF or NULL when an error occurs. Other library routines usually return either −1 or 0 on error (depending on what the type of their return value is), although some routines may return different values indicating one of several different errors. Unlike library routines, system calls are identical in the way they indicate that an error has occurred. Every system call returns the value −1 when an error occurs, and most return 0 on successful completion (unless they are returning some other integer value). Further, the external integer errno is set to a number indicating exactly which error occurred. The "values" of these errors are defined in the include file *errno.h*, and may be easily printed out using the perror library routine (described in Chapter 14, *Miscellaneous Routines*).

In newer versions of UNIX such as System V and 4.3BSD, the Standard I/O (stdio) routines all set errno properly so that perror can be used in conjunction with them. Unfortunately, earlier versions of stdio did not properly set errno. perror cannot be used with these earlier routines.

Errors are important. Good programs are those that do not die a horrible death in the face of an unexpected error. The idea behind this is simply Murphy's Law: if anything can go wrong, it will. Programs should be prepared for this inevitability by checking the return codes from all system calls and library routines whose failure will cause problems.

Nonetheless, in order to save space and emphasize the important parts of the code, many of the examples in this book do not always check return codes as should be done in real life. The examples should be taken as demonstrations of the functions being discussed, not as complete examples of good UNIX programming practice.

2

The Standard
I/O Library

File Pointers
Opening and Creating Files
Closing Files
Reading and Writing Files
Moving Around in Files

A programmer learning C is usually taught to use the routines in the Standard I/O Library (stdio)* to perform input and output (I/O). These routines perform so-called *high-level* input and output. That is, the routines perform three important functions for the programmer:

- Buffering is performed automatically. Rather than reading or writing data a few bytes at a time, the routines perform the actual input or output in large "chunks" of several thousand bytes at a time. (The size of the buffer is generally specified by the constant BUFSIZ, defined in the include file *stdio.h*.) The routines *seem* to read or write in small units, but the data is actually saved in a buffer. This buffering is internal to the routines, and is invisible to the programmer.

- Input and output conversions are performed. For example, when using the printf routine to print an integer (with %d), the *character representation* of that integer is actually printed. Similarly, when using scanf, the character representation of an integer is converted into its numeric value.

---

*Pronounced "stŭdīo"

- Input and output are automatically formatted. That is, it is possible to use field widths and the like to print numbers and strings in any desired format.

This chapter provides a review of the more commonly used routines contained in the Standard I/O Library.

File Pointers

In the Standard I/O Library, a file is called a *stream*, and is described by a pointer to an object of type FILE, called a *file pointer*. The FILE data type is defined in the include file *stdio.h*, which should be included before using any of the stdio routines. There are three predefined file pointers, stdin, stdout, and stderr. These refer to the standard input (keyboard), standard output (terminal screen), and standard error output, respectively.

Most of the stdio routines require that a file pointer referring to an open stream be passed to them. However, when reading from the standard input or writing to the standard output, stdio provides "shorthand" routines that assume one of these streams rather than requiring them to be specified. Table 2-1 shows these routines and their equivalents.

Table 2-1. Shorthand routines for standard input and output.

Shorthand	Equivalent
getchar()	fgetc(stdin), getc(stdin)
gets(*buf*)	fgets(*buf*, BUFSIZ, stdin)
printf(*args*)	fprintf(stdout, *args*)
putchar(*c*)	fputc(*c*, stdout), putc(*c*, stdout)
puts(*buf*)	fputs(*buf*, stdout)
scanf(*args*)	fscanf(stdin, *args*)

Opening and Creating Files

In order to read from or write to a file, that file must first be opened for reading or writing (or both). The fopen routine is used for this purpose. fopen takes two arguments: a character string containing the name of the file to open, and a character string describing how that file should be opened. It returns a pointer to an open stream of type FILE, or the constant NULL if the file could not be opened.

The second argument to fopen may take on one of the following values:

r   The file will be opened for reading only. The file must already exist if this is to succeed.

w   The file will be opened for writing only. If the file does not exist, it will be created as an empty file. If the file does exist, the contents of the file will be destroyed.

a   The file will be opened for writing only. If the file does not exist, it will be created as an empty file. However, if the file does exist, the contents of that file will *not* be destroyed. Instead, any data written to the file will be appended to the end, rather than overwriting the existing data.

Additionally, a plus sign (+) may be appended to one of the above letters, causing the file to be opened for both reading and writing. Note however that specifying r+ requires that the file already exist and does not destroy any data in the file, while specifying w+ or a+ will create the file if it does not exist.*

Closing Files

The fclose routine is used to close an open stream. fclose takes a single argument, the file pointer referring to the stream to be closed. When called, this routine flushes the buffers for the stream, and performs some other internal cleanup functions. 0 is returned on success; the constant EOF is returned if an error occurs.

Reading and Writing Files

The Standard I/O Library provides several ways to read and write data to and from a file.

---

*Some older versions of the Standard I/O Library do not support the "+" mechanism. All versions of the library currently being sold do support it, however.

The getc and putc Routines

The simplest way to read and write data is one character (byte) at a time. This is done by using the getc and putc routines. getc accepts a single argument, a file pointer referring to a stream open for reading. It returns the next character read from that stream, or the constant EOF when the end of the file has been reached. putc accepts two arguments, a character to be written, and a file pointer referring to a stream open for writing. It places that character onto the stream and returns 0 if it succeeds, or EOF if an error occurs.

It is important to note here that although getc and putc process one character at a time, the stdio library routines do not actually issue system calls to read and write from the disk each time the routines are called. Instead, the library buffers these characters internally, and only issues a system call once every several thousand characters. Thus, processing even extremely large files is still very efficient.

Example 2-1 shows a small program that appends one file onto another. The first argument specifies the name of the file to be copied, and the second file specifies the name of a file to be appended to. If the file to be appended to does not exist, it will be created.

Example 2-1. append-char—append one file to another character by character

```
#include <stdio.h>

main(argc, argv)
int argc;
char **argv;
{
    int c;
    FILE *from, *to;

    /*
     * Check our arguments.
     */
    if (argc != 3) {
        fprintf(stderr, "Usage: %s from-file to-file\n", *argv);
        exit(1);
    }

    /*
     * Open the from-file for reading.
     */
    if ((from = fopen(argv[1], "r")) == NULL) {
        perror(argv[1]);
        exit(1);
    }
```

```
/*
 * Open the to-file for appending.  If to-file does
 * not exist, fopen will create it.
 */
if ((to = fopen(argv[2], "a")) == NULL) {
    perror(argv[2]);
    exit(1);
}

/*
 * Now read characters from from-file until we
 * hit end-of-file, and put them onto to-file.
 */
while ((c = getc(from)) != EOF)
    putc(c, to);

/*
 * Now close the files.
 */
fclose(from);
fclose(to);
exit(0);
}
```

For brevity, and to emphasize the information being discussed in this chapter, Example 2-1 (and the following examples) violates one of the more important UNIX conventions. This convention dictates that in any program where it makes sense, the program should operate on both named files, or on its standard input and output. The text formatting programs *tbl*, *eqn*, *nroff*, and *troff* are good examples of programs that do this. Given a list of filenames, these programs will open the files and process the data in them. However, if no filenames are given, these programs will read data from their standard input. This allows the programs to operate as filters, so that they can be invoked individually or as part of a pipeline (see Chapter 9, *Executing Programs*).

The fgets and fputs Routines

Another way to read and write files provided by the Standard I/O Library allows the programmer to process data a line at a time. A line is defined as a string of zero or more characters terminated by a new-line character. The fgets function accepts three arguments: a pointer to a character buffer to be filled, an integer specifying the size of the buffer, and a file pointer referring to a stream open for reading. A pointer to the filled buffer is returned on success, or the constant NULL is returned when end-of-file is reached. The buffer will be filled with one line of characters, including the new-line character, and will be terminated with a null character. fputs accepts two arguments, a pointer to a null-terminated string of characters, and a file pointer referring to a stream open for writing. It returns 0 on success, or the constant EOF if an error occurs.

Example 2-2 shows another version of our program to append one file to another; this version does it a line at a time. The constant BUFSIZ is defined in the include file *stdio.h*, and is configured to be an optimum size for the system. Unless you need a particular size, this is a good value to use whenever you are working with stdio.

Example 2-2. append-line—append one file to another line by line

```
#include <stdio.h>

main(argc, argv)
int argc;
char **argv;
{
    FILE *from, *to;
    char line[BUFSIZ];

    /*
     * Check our arguments.
     */
    if (argc != 3) {
        fprintf(stderr, "Usage: %s from-file to-file\n", *argv);
        exit(1);
    }

    /*
     * Open the from-file for reading.
     */
    if ((from = fopen(argv[1], "r")) == NULL) {
        perror(argv[1]);
        exit(1);
    }

    /*
     * Open the to-file for appending.  If to-file does
     * not exist, fopen will create it.
     */
    if ((to = fopen(argv[2], "a")) == NULL) {
        perror(argv[2]);
        exit(1);
    }

    /*
     * Now read a line at a time from the from-file,
     * and write it to the to-file.
     */
    while (fgets(line, BUFSIZ, from) != NULL)
        fputs(line, to);

    /*
```

```
     * Now close the files.
     */
    fclose(from);
    fclose(to);
    exit(0);
}
```

The fread and fwrite Routines

The Standard I/O Library also provides a method to read and write data without dividing it up into characters or lines. This is usually desirable when working with files that do not consist only of text, but also include arbitrary binary data. The `fread` function accepts four arguments: a pointer to an array of some data type (characters, integers, structures, etc.), an integer indicating the size of one array element in bytes, an integer indicating the number of array elements to read, and a file pointer referring to a stream open for reading. It returns the number of array elements actually read in, or 0 on end-of-file. The `fwrite` function also accepts four arguments, as described above for `fread`. It returns the number of array elements actually written, or 0 on error.

The advantage to using a routine like `fread` or `fwrite` lies primarily in the ability to impose a structure on the input or output stream not provided by the stdio routines themselves. For example, if a file contains 100 binary floating-point numbers, the easiest way to read these in would be to use something like the code segment shown below:

```
FILE *fp;
float numbers[100];

.....

fread(numbers, sizeof(float), 100, fp);

.....
```

Example 2-3 shows still another version of our file appending program; this version copies the data a buffer-full of characters at a time.

Example 2-3. append-buf—append one file to another a buffer-full at a time

```
#include <stdio.h>

main(argc, argv)
int argc;
char **argv;
{
    int n;
```

```
    FILE *from, *to;
    char buf[BUFSIZ];

    /*
     * Check our arguments.
     */
    if (argc != 3) {
        fprintf(stderr, "Usage: %s from-file to-file\n", *argv);
        exit(1);
    }

    /*
     * Open the from-file for reading.
     */
    if ((from = fopen(argv[1], "r")) == NULL) {
        perror(argv[1]);
        exit(1);
    }

    /*
     * Open the to-file for appending.  If to-file does
     * not exist, fopen will create it.
     */
    if ((to = fopen(argv[2], "a")) == NULL) {
        perror(argv[2]);
        exit(1);
    }

    /*
     * Note that we only write the number of characters fread
     * read in, rather than always writing BUFSIZ characters.
     */
    while ((n = fread(buf, sizeof(char), BUFSIZ, from)) > 0)
        fwrite(buf, sizeof(char), n, to);

    /*
     * Now close the files.
     */
    fclose(from);
    fclose(to);
    exit(0);
}
```

The fscanf and fprintf Routines

Other than dividing data into units of characters or lines, the routines described in the previous sections do not interpret the data they manipulate. Sometimes however, more interpretation of the data is necessary.

As you probably know, the internal representation of data in the computer is not generally human-readable. For example, the number 10 is represented internally as a series of (usually) 32 bits:

```
00000000000000000000000000001010
```

However, when this number is to be printed on a line printer or terminal screen, it must be converted to the two ASCII characters '1' and '0', which have completely different bit patterns:

```
1:      00110001
0:      00110000
```

Likewise, in order to read in a number from the keyboard, the characters that represent that number to a human must be converted into the internal representation of that number in order for the computer to deal with it.

The fscanf routine accepts a variable number of arguments. The first argument is a file pointer referring to a stream open for reading. The second argument is a character string that specifies the format of the input data. The rest of the arguments are pointers to the data objects that are to be filled. fscanf reads characters from the stream, converts them into various internal representations as specified by the format string, and stores them in the data objects.

The format string may contain:

• Blanks, tabs, and new-line characters, which match optional white space in the input.

• An ordinary character (other than '%'), which must match the next input character.

• A conversion specification, consisting of a '%' character followed by a conversion character.

A conversion specification indicates how the next input field is to be interpreted; the result is placed in the corresponding argument. Some of the more common conversion characters are:*

d   A decimal integer is expected; the corresponding argument should be a pointer to an integer.

f   A floating-point number is expected; the corresponding argument should be a pointer to an object of type float.

---

*See the manual for the complete list.

s   A character string is expected; the corresponding argument should point to a character array large enough to hold the string plus a terminating null character. The input field is terminated by a space or new-line character.

For example, to read in the string:

```
123 Hello 45.678
```

the call:

```
fscanf("%d %s %f", &intvar, stringvar, &floatvar)
```

could be used. `fscanf` returns the number of input items matched, or the constant `EOF` when end-of-file has been reached.

The `fprintf` routine also accepts a variable number of arguments. The first argument is a file pointer to a stream open for writing, the second is again a format string, and the following arguments are the objects to be printed. Ordinary (non-'%') characters in the format string are copied to the output stream. A '%' character specifies that the corresponding argument is to be converted; the conversion characters are the same as those described for `fscanf`.

Example 2-4 shows a small program that asks you to enter a number, and then computes the factorial of that number and prints it out. This example uses the `printf` and `scanf` routines, which assume the use of the streams `stdout` and `stdin`, rather than requiring the streams to be passed as arguments.

Example 2-4. factorial—compute the factorial of a number

```
#include <stdio.h>

main()
{
    int n, m;

    printf("Enter a number: ");
    scanf("%d", &n);

    m = fact(n);

    printf("The factorial of %d is %d.\n", n, m);
    exit(0);
}

fact(n)
int n;
{
```

```
if (n == 0)
    return(1);

return(n * fact(n-1));
}
```

The sscanf and sprintf Routines

Stdio also provides the ability to "print" formatted data into a character string, and to "read" formatted data from a character string. The sscanf and sprintf routines are identical to fscanf and fprintf, except that instead of taking a file pointer as their first argument, they take a character string. sscanf will copy characters from the character string, converting them according to its second argument. sprintf will place a formatted copy of its arguments into the character string. The uses of these functions are endless.

Moving Around in Files

It is often necessary to move to a specific location in a file before reading or writing data. For example, if a file contains several fixed-size items indexed by number, it may be easier to skip over unwanted records to read or write the desired record, rather than reading and processing all the records preceding the desired one.

The Standard I/O Library routine for moving around in a file is called fseek. It accepts three arguments: a file pointer to an open stream, a long integer specifying the number of bytes to move, called an *offset*, and an integer indicating from where in the file the offset is to be taken. If the third argument is 0, the offset is taken from the beginning of the file. If it is 1, the offset is taken from the current location in the file. If the third argument is 2, the offset is taken from the end of the file.

To move to the end of a file, the call:

```
fseek(fp, 0L, 2)
```

should be used.* To move to the beginning of the file, the call:

```
fseek(fp, 0L, 0)
```

may be used, or equivalently, the rewind routine may be used. rewind takes a single argument, a file pointer to an open stream.

---

*An integer followed by an 'L' indicates a *long* integer to the C compiler.

To find out the current location in a file, the `ftell` routine should be used. `ftell` accepts a single argument, a file pointer to an open stream, and returns a long integer indicating the offset from the beginning of the file.

Example 2-5 shows a small program that creates a data file with one record for each of five users. In order to demonstrate the use of `fseek`, the program writes the file backwards; that is, the last record is written first, and the first record is written last. This is somewhat pointless in practice, but serves to demonstrate the appropriate concepts. You should enter this program and execute it. Then try to write a program that will read the records from the file in the order 3, 0, 2, 1, 4 and print them out.*

Example 2-5. fseekdemo—demonstrate the use of the fseek routine

```
/*
 *
 */
#include <stdio.h>

struct record {
    int uid;
    char login[9];
};

char *logins[] = { "user1", "user2", "user3",
                   "user4", "user5" };

main()
{
    int i;
    FILE *fp;
    struct record rec;

    /*
     * Open the data file for writing.
     */
    if ((fp = fopen("datafile", "w")) == NULL) {
        perror("datafile");
        exit(1);
    }

    /*
     * For each user, going backwards...
     */
    for (i=4; i >= 0; i--) {
        /*
         * Create the record.
```

---

*HINT: change the `fwrite` to `fread` in the `putrec` function, and then call it with each of the values above. Don't forget to change the call to `fopen` to open the file for reading.

```
           */
          rec.uid = i;
          strcpy(rec.login, logins[i]);

          /*
           * Output the record.  Notice we pass the
           * address of the structure.
           */
          putrec(fp, i, &rec);
     }

     fclose(fp);
     exit(0);
}

/*
 * putrec--write the record in the i'th position.
 */
putrec(fp, i, r)
int i;
FILE *fp;
struct record *r;
{
     /*
      * Seek to the i'th position from the beginning
      * of the file.
      */
     fseek(fp, (long) i * sizeof(struct record), 0);

     /*
      * Write the record.  We want to write one
      * object the size of a record structure.
      */
     fwrite((char *) r, sizeof(struct record), 1, fp);
}
```

3

Low-level I/O

File Descriptors
Opening and Creating Files
Closing Files
Reading and Writing Files
Moving Around in Files
Converting File Descriptors to File
    Pointers

As discussed in the previous chapter, the Standard I/O Library provides a wealth of different methods for reading and writing data efficiently and easily. However, the tasks performed by these routines, namely buffering and input/output conversion, are not always desirable. For example, when performing input and output directly to and from a device such as a tape drive, the programmer needs to be able to determine the buffer sizes to be used, rather than letting the stdio routines do it.

And of course, routines do exist that provide that level of control. The Standard I/O Library is simply a user-friendly interface to the system calls described in this chapter, which we will call the *low-level* interface.

File Descriptors

Recall that in the Standard I/O Library, a file is referred to by a file pointer. When using the low-level interface, a file is referred to using a *file descriptor*, which is simply a small integer. As with stdio, there are three predefined file descriptors,

0, 1, and 2, which refer to the standard input, standard output, and standard error output respectively.

Unlike the Standard I/O Library, which provides a "shorthand" set of routines to deal with the standard input and output, all the low-level I/O routines require that a valid file descriptor be passed to them.

Opening and Creating Files

The open routine is used to open a file for reading and/or writing, or to create it. open takes three arguments: a character string containing the name of the file to open, an integer specifying how the file is to be opened, and an integer *mode* for use when creating a file (see below). It returns an integer file descriptor on success, or –1 if the file could not be opened. The second argument to open is made up of various constants ORed together. These constants, shown below, are defined in the include file *sys/file.h* on Berkeley systems, and *sys/fcntl.h* on System V systems:

O_RDONLY   Open the file for reading only.

O_WRONLY   Open the file for writing only.

O_RDWR   Open the file for reading and writing.

O_APPEND   Append to the file when writing, rather than starting at the beginning.

O_CREAT   Create the file if it does not exist. The mode should be given as the third argument.

O_TRUNC   Truncate the file to zero length if opened for writing.

O_EXCL   Return error if the file is to be created and already exists.

O_NDELAY   Do not block on open. (This will be explained later.)

If the O_CREAT option is given, the third argument should contain the mode with which the file should be created. This mode specifies the access permissions on the file, and is described in more detail in Chapter 4, *Files and Directories*.

Opening and Creating Files on Older UNIX Systems

On pre-4.2BSD and pre-System V versions of UNIX, the open system call only accepts two arguments, a character string containing the name of the file to be opened, and an integer indicating how the file is to be opened. If the integer is equal to 0 the file is opened for reading, if it is equal to 1 the file is opened for writing, and if it is equal to 2 the file is opened for reading and writing. If the file does not exist, the open fails, and –1 is returned.

The `creat` system call is used to create a file. This call also accepts two arguments, the name of the file to be created, and the mode with which to create the file. If the call succeeds, a file descriptor open for writing is returned, otherwise –1 is returned.

Note that there is no facility to open the file for appending—the `lseek` system call (see below) must be used to move to the end of the file in order to do this.

Closing Files

The `close` system call is used to close an open file. `close` takes a single argument, the file descriptor referring to the file to be closed. 0 is returned on success; –1 is returned if an error occurs.

Reading and Writing Files

Now that we can open and close files, the next thing to do is read and write data to and from that file. There is only one way to read from a file using the low-level interface, and likewise, only one way to write to a file—a buffer-full at a time.

The size of the buffer is left up to the programmer, and it is his or her responsibility to use an appropriate value. For example, if the programmer reads or writes characters one at a time, instead of in units of a few thousand, the operating system will access the disk (or other device) once for each character (and the program will run very slowly!).*

The `read` system call takes three arguments; a file descriptor open for reading, a pointer to a buffer of data to be filled, and an integer indicating the number of bytes to be read. It returns the number of bytes actually read, or –1 on error. If end-of-file has been reached, 0 is returned.

The `write` system call also takes three arguments: a file descriptor open for writing, a pointer to a buffer of data to be written, and an integer indicating the number of bytes to be written. It returns the number of bytes actually written, or –1 on error.

---

*Actually, this is not strictly true since I/O to some devices is buffered internally by the operating system.

Example 3-1 shows a low-level version of our file appending program. Note that because `read` and `write` cause the system to access the disk each time they are called, it is important for the programmer to specify reasonably large buffer sizes or else his or her program (and the system) will run very slowly. Try experimenting with large and small buffer sizes to get a feel for the difference (you may need to use a file of five or ten thousand characters to really appreciate the difference).

Example 3-1. append-ll—append one file to another using the low-level interface

```c
/* Change <sys/file.h> to <sys/fcntl.h> if you're on System V.
 */
#include <sys/file.h>

main(argc, argv)
int argc;
char **argv;
{
    int n;
    int from, to;
    char buf[1024];

    /*
     * Check our arguments.  Note that to write the error
     * message we can't just use "%s" as we did in Example
     * 2-3; we have to write each string separately.
     */
    if (argc != 3) {
        write(2, "Usage: ", 7);
        write(2, *argv, strlen(*argv));
        write(2, " from-file to-file\n", 19);
        exit(1);
    }

    /*
     * Open the from-file for reading.
     */
    if ((from = open(argv[1], O_RDONLY)) < 0) {
        perror(argv[1]);
        exit(1);
    }

    /*
     * Open the to-file for appending.  If to-file does
     * not exist, open will create it with mode 644
     * (-rw-r--r--).  Note that we specify the mode
     * in octal, not decimal
     */
    if ((to = open(argv[2], O_WRONLY|O_CREAT|O_APPEND, 0644)) < 0) {
        perror(argv[2]);
        exit(1);
```

```
    }

    /*
     * Now read a buffer-full at a time from the from-file,
     * and write it to the to-file.  Note that we only
     * write the number of characters read read in,
     * rather than always writing 1024 characters.
     */
    while ((n = read(from, buf, sizeof(buf))) > 0)
        write(to, buf, n);

    /*
     * Now close the files.
     */
    close(from);
    close(to);
    exit(0);
}
```

Moving Around in Files

As mentioned before, it is often necessary to move to a specific location in a file before reading or writing data.

The low-level routine for moving around in a file is called lseek. Like the stdio fseek, it accepts three arguments: a file descriptor to an open file, a long integer specifying the number of bytes to move, called an *offset*, and an integer indicating from where in the file the offset is to be taken. The third argument is usually specified as one of the constants defined in *sys/file.h* on Berkeley UNIX or *sys/fcntl.h* on System V. On older systems, these constants are not defined, and the values shown in parentheses below should be used instead.

If the third argument is L_SET (0), the offset is taken from the beginning of the file. If it is L_INCR (1), the offset is taken from the current location in the file. Finally, if the third argument is L_XTND (2), the offset is taken from the end of the file. lseek returns the new offset from the beginning of the file.

To move to the end of a file, the call:

```
    lseek(fd, 0L, L_XTND)
```

should be used. To move to the beginning of the file, the call:

```
    lseek(fd, 0L, L_SET)
```

may be used. There is no low-level rewind routine.

To find out the current location in a file, the call:

```
lseek(fd, 0L, L_INCR)
```

should be used. This tells `lseek` to move zero places away from the current location in the file, and `lseek` will return the "new" offset. There is no low-level `ftell` routine.

Example 3-2 shows the low-level version of Example 2-5, which wrote records for each of five users. Note the similarities between the two programs. As before, you should enter this program and execute it. Then try to write a program that will read the records from the file in the order 3, 0, 2, 1, 4 and print them out.

Example 3-2. lseekdemo—demonstrate the use of the `lseek` *system call*

```
/*
 * If you're on System V, change <sys/file.h> to <sys/fcntl.h>.
 */
#include <sys/file.h>

struct record {
    int uid;
    char login[9];
};

char *logins[] = { "user1", "user2", "user3",
                   "user4", "user5" };

main()
{
    int i, fd;
    struct record rec;

    /*
     * Open the data file for writing.
     */
    if ((fd = open("datafile", O_WRONLY | O_CREAT, 0644)) < 0) {
        perror("datafile");
        exit(1);
    }

    /*
     * For each user, going backwards...
     */
    for (i=4; i >= 0; i--) {
        /*
         * Create the record.
         */
        rec.uid = i;
        strcpy(rec.login, logins[i]);

        /*
```

```
              * Output the record.  Notice we pass the
              * address of the structure.
              */
             putrec(fd, i, &rec);
        }

        close(fd);
        exit(0);
    }

    /*
     * putrec--write the record in the i'th position.
     */
    putrec(fd, i, r)
    int i, fd;
    struct record *r;
    {
        /*
         * Seek to the i'th position from the beginning
         * of the file.
         */
        lseek(fd, (long) i * sizeof(struct record), L_SET);

        /*
         * Write the record.  We want to write one
         * object the size of a record structure.
         */
        write(fd, (char *) r, sizeof(struct record));
    }
```

Duplicating File Descriptors

Occasionally it is necessary to have more than one file descriptor referring to the same file. This is common when forking and executing new processes.* To obtain a new file descriptor which refers to the same file that fd does, the call:

```
    fd2 = dup(fd)
```

should be used. fd2 will now refer to the same file, and will be at the same position in the file as fd. dup returns –1 if an error occurs.

An alternate form of the call allows the programmer to select which file descriptor he or she wishes to refer to the file. For example, suppose that standard input should be connected to a given disk file referred to by fd (this is how the shell handles the '<' redirect). The call:

---

*See Chapter 9, *Executing Programs*.

```
dup2(fd, 0)
```

will cause file descriptor 0 to be closed if in use, and then joined to the file to which `fd` refers. This call is not available in System V, where it has been replaced by `fcntl` (described in Chapter 4, *Files and Directories*). Berkeley UNIX has both `dup2` and `fcntl`.†

A fairly common code segment seen in UNIX source code looks like:

```
close(0);
dup(fd);
```

This tends to confuse new programmers, since it appears that the return value from `dup` is being ignored. Actually, the program is relying on a feature of the UNIX system which says that a file descriptor is always allocated as the lowest-numbered available descriptor. Thus, in the segment above, since the file descriptor 0 was just closed, it will be allocated on the `dup` call, thus effectively performing exactly the same task as the call to `dup2`, above. This practice of relying on operating system internals is arguably poor; however it does occur often in the real world.

Converting File Descriptors to File Pointers

Sometimes it is desirable to convert an existing low-level file descriptor referring to an open file into something that can be used with the Standard I/O Library. For example, the `pipe` system call, described in Chapter 9, returns a file descriptor connected to the output stream of another program. If this program prints nothing but a list of numbers, it would be useful to be able to use `fscanf` to read them in.

The stdio routine `fdopen` takes two arguments: a file descriptor referring to an open file, and a character string indicating how the file descriptor is to be used. This second argument is exactly identical to the second argument used with `fopen`. `fdopen` returns a file pointer whose stream refers to the same file as the file descriptor, or the constant `NULL` on failure.

---

†Because the POSIX standard specifies it, `dup2` has been returned in System V Release 3.0.

4

Files and Directories

File System Concepts
Determining the Accessibility of a File
Getting Information from an I-Node
Reading Directories
Modifying File Attributes
Miscellaneous File System Routines

File System Concepts

Before describing the many system calls and library routines available for manipulating files and directories, it is necessary to provide a brief overview of the UNIX file system.

Ordinary Files

A file contains whatever information a user places in it. Unlike other operating systems, no format is imposed on a regular file (e.g., sequential, random access, etc.). Instead, a regular file is considered simply as a sequence of bytes, and these bytes may be read and written in any way the programmer desires. Certain programs expect a file to be in a specific format; for example the assembler generates an object file in a specific format, and the loader expects that format as input. The important feature to note is that the structure of files is controlled by the programs that access them, not by the operating system.

Directories

Directories provide the mapping between the names of files and the files themselves, thus inducing a structure on the file system as a whole. A directory contains a number of files; it may also contain subdirectories which in turn contain more files. A directory behaves exactly like an ordinary file when read, though it may not be written by unprivileged (non-super-user) programs.

The operating system maintains several directories for its own use; one of these is the *root* directory. All files in the file system can be found by tracing a path through a chain of directories starting at the root until the desired file is reached.

When the name of a file is specified to the system, it may be in the form of a *path name*, which is a sequence of filenames separated by slashes. Any filename but the one following the last slash must be the name of a directory. If the sequence begins with a slash, the search begins in the root directory; otherwise the search begins in the program's current directory. As limiting cases, the name "/" refers to the root directory and a null filename (e.g., */a/b/*) refers to the directory whose name precedes it. Two slashes together ("//") are interpreted as a single slash.

Each directory always has at least two entries.* The name "." in each directory refers to the directory itself. Thus a program may read its current directory, without knowing its name, by opening the file ".". By convention, the name ".." refers to the parent of the directory in which it appears, that is, to the directory in which the current directory was created. A program may move from its current directory to the root directory by constantly changing its directory to "..". As a limiting case, when in the root directory the name ".." is a circular link to the root.

Special Files

Special files are one of the most unusual aspects of the UNIX file system. Each I/O device (disk drive, tape drive, terminal, etc.) is associated with at least one such file. To user programs, special files look just like any other file,† but requests to read or write the file result in activation of the associated device. For example, a program wishing to write on a magnetic tape might open the file */dev/mt* . Requests to read and write this file will cause the tape to move and data to be read or written at the appropriate density, etc. By a long-standing UNIX convention, entries for special files reside in the directory */dev* , but there is nothing in the operating system that requires or enforces this.

---

*This is not actually a requirement, but is true unless the directory is created in an unusual fashion.
†This is not strictly true, but for the purposes of this discussion it is accurate enough.

Removable File Systems

It is not necessary that the entire file system hierarchy be stored on the same device, even though the root of the file system always resides in the same place (so that it may be located at system startup time). The mount system call (and the associated user command) takes two arguments: the name of a special file whose associated storage volume (e.g., a disk pack) has the structure of an independent file system containing its own directory hierarchy, and the name of an existing (ordinary) file or directory. The effect of this call is to replace a leaf of the directory tree with the subtree stored on the special file. All references to the (previously) ordinary file or directory now cause a reference to the tree stored on the new device. Note that the concept of files and directories must be preserved when mounting; a directory tree cannot be mounted on a file and vice versa.

A slight problem exists with terminology here—the entire directory hierarchy, starting with the root, is technically what is termed the file system. However, in common usage, each mounted directory tree is also referred to as a file system. Thus the definition becomes recursive—"the file system is composed of files, directories, and mounted file systems." Fortunately, however, it is usually easy to infer which meaning is intended from the context in which it is used.

Device Numbers

Each special file on the system is associated with two device numbers. The *major device number* informs the operating system which device type is to be used when the filename is referenced. Each type of device has an operating system-resident section of code called a "device driver" which operates on that type of device. The *minor device number* is passed to the device driver. This number is used to determine which physical device is to be used. For example, the minor device number is used to determine which disk drive on a multiple-drive controller is to be accessed, which partition of a disk drive is to be used, or if a tape drive should be rewound when the requested operation has been completed. Several devices (e.g., disk drives of the same type) may have the same major device number, but they will all have different minor device numbers. (The method for obtaining the major and minor device numbers of a special file will be described shortly.)

I-Numbers, the I-List, and I-Nodes

As mentioned above, directories provide the mapping between the names of files and the files themselves. A directory is made up of a series of structures; each structure contains the name of a file and a pointer to the file itself. This pointer is an integer called the *i-number* (for index number) of the file. When the file is accessed, its i-number is used as an index into a system table (the *i-list*) where the entry for the file (the *i-node*) is stored. The i-node contains a description of the file:

- The user and group ids of its owner.
- Its protection.
- The physical disk addresses for the file contents.
- Its size.
- Time of last inode change, last use, and last modification.
- The number of links to the file; that is, the number of times it appears in directories.
- A tag indicating the file type (directory, regular file, or special file).

The system maintains a separate i-list for each mounted directory tree; thus, it is possible for several files in the file system to have the same i-number. By using the major and minor device numbers associated with the special file of the directory tree in conjunction with an i-number, each file in the file system can be uniquely determined.*

Hard Links

It is possible to have more than one name refer to the same file by making a *link* to that file. This link is handled in the file system simply by making a new entry in the directory with the new name and the i-number of the file. This type of link is commonly called a *hard link*. Note that because i-numbers are not unique across file systems, it is not possible to link across them. It is possible, though, to have the same file referred to in different directories on the same file system; for example */a/b/c* and */a/d/e/f* may be links to the same file. Regardless of how many hard links there are to a file, though, there is still only one inode describing that file.

---

*This unfortunately breaks down somewhat when using networked file systems. With a networked file system, it is also necessary to know which machine the file is stored on if a file is to be uniquely determined.

Symbolic Links

In 4.2BSD, a new type of file called a *symbolic link* was introduced. A symbolic link acts as a pointer to another file (its link). This is accomplished in the file system by creating a file with the link's name which contains the path name of the file the link points to. Because i-numbers are not involved in symbolic links, these links may be used to link across mounted file systems. This provides an extra degree of flexibility (at a very minor cost in speed) that hard links do not provide.

A different way to explain the difference between hard links and symbolic links is to say that because symbolic links are not evaluated until *run time*, they are more flexible. But because hard links are evaluated at *link time*, they require less processing time.

Because some of the more advanced parts of the file system, as well as some of the finer details of the system in general, have not been covered here, this description is far from complete. However, it should provide you with enough of an idea of the structure of the UNIX file system to follow the discussion in the remaining sections of this chapter.

Determining the Accessibility of a File

To determine if a file is accessible to a program, the `access` system call may be used. This call takes two arguments: the first is a character string containing the path name to the file in question, the second is a small integer. The integer's value determines which access permission is to be checked, and is specified as one of the constants defined in *sys/file.h* : `F_OK` for existence of the file, `X_OK` for execute (search) access, `W_OK` for write access, and `R_OK` for read access.* These values may be ORed together to check for more than one access permission. The call returns 0 if the program has the given access permissions, otherwise −1 is returned and `errno` is set to the reason for failure. This call is somewhat useful in that it makes checking for a specific permission easy. However, it only answers the question "do I have this permission?" It cannot answer the question "what permissions do I have?"

---

*On older systems, these constants are not defined, and the values 0, 1, 2, and 4, respectively, should be used instead.

Getting Information from an I-Node

The system call used for obtaining the information stored in an i-node is called stat. It takes two arguments: a character string containing the name of the file of interest, and a pointer to a structure of type stat. An alternative form of the call, fstat, takes an open file descriptor in place of the character string;† information is given about the file referred to by the file descriptor. 4.2BSD added a third form of the call, lstat, which is used with symbolic links. Simply, stat follows symbolic links providing information about what they point to, while lstat provides information about the link itself. The calls are identical when used on other types of files. All the calls return 0 on success and −1 on failure; setting the errno variable to the error condition.

The stat structure is defined in the include file *sys/stat.h*, along with several constants. The file *sys/types.h* must also be included, to provide the type definitions used in the structure. The stat structure varies slightly among different versions (and different ports) of UNIX. There is however, a common set of structure elements present in all versions of the structure. These are shown below:

```
struct stat {
    dev_t      st_dev;
    ino_t      st_ino;
    u_short    st_mode;
    short      st_nlink;
    short      st_uid;
    short      st_gid;
    dev_t      st_rdev;
    off_t      st_size;
    time_t     st_atime;
    time_t     st_mtime;
    time_t     st_ctime;
};
```

The elements of this structure serve the following purposes:

st_dev   The major and minor device numbers of the device which the i-node is stored on. These are stored in either half of the word, and may be accessed using the major and minor macros defined in *sys/types.h*.

---

†Note that this is counter-intuitive: other I/O routines whose name starts with "f" expect a file pointer; this one expects the low-level file descriptor.

st_ino   The i-node number.

st_mode   A set of bits encoding the type of file and the access permissions it has.

st_nlink The number of hard links to the file, including the file itself (a file with no links will have the value 1 in this field). Symbolic links to the file are not counted here (nor anywhere else).

st_uid   The user id of the owner of the file.

st_gid   The group id of the file (for permission checks).

st_rdev   The type of device if the i-node is that of a device (special) file.

st_size   The size of the file in bytes.

st_atime   The last time the file was accessed (read or executed), stored in standard UNIX time format.*

st_mtime   The last time the file was modified (written).

st_ctime   The last time the i-node was changed. This time is updated whenever the file's mode is changed, the file's access or modification times are updated, etc. This is *not* the file's creation time, as many programs and documents incorrectly state.

Most of these fields are relatively self-explanatory, and are usually just used "as is" by the programs which deal with them. However, the st_mode field is important in that it contains both the type and mode of the file. This information is extracted from this field by ANDing the value stored there with various constants defined in *sys/stat.h*:

S_IFMT   This constant extracts the type bits from the mode word. The mode should be ANDed with this, and then compared against the various type constants:

        S_IFDIR   Directory.

        S_IFCHR   Character special (raw) device.

        S_IFBLK   Block special (buffered) device.

        S_IFREG   Regular file.

        S_IFMPC   Multiplexed character special (Version 7 only).

        S_IFMPB   Multiplexed block special (Version 7 only).

        S_IFLNK   Symbolic link (Berkeley UNIX only).

---

*See Chapter 7, *Telling Time and Timing Things*.

S_IFSOCK	Socket (Berkeley UNIX only).
S_IFIFO	FIFO buffer (System V only).

S_ISUID   If the result of ANDing this bit with the mode is non-zero, the file has the set-user-id bit set.

S_ISGID   If the result of ANDing this bit with the mode is non-zero, the file has the set-group-id bit set.

S_ISVTX   If the result of ANDing this bit with the mode is non-zero, the file has the "sticky bit" set. This means that the text of the program (the bit is meaningless on non-program files) will be saved on the swap disk even though nobody is running it. This idea came about under Version 6 UNIX on the PDP-11 to make often-used programs load faster; with the onset of paging systems it is more or less obsolete.

S_IREAD   By ANDing this value directly with the mode, it may be determined if the owner of the file has read permission (if the result of the operation is non-zero). By shifting the constant to the right 3 places (or shifting the mode left 3 places) and ANDing, the group read permission may be checked. By shifting six places, world read permission may be checked.

S_IWRITE   Like S_IREAD, this bit checks the write permissions on the file.

S_IEXEC   Like S_IREAD, this bit checks the execute permissions on the file if it is a non-directory file. If the file is a directory, this bit implies permission to search the directory (i.e., access files contained in the directory).

Don't worry if the previous pages seem a little overwhelming. After the next section on reading directories, an example program will be presented which looks like the standard system program *ls*. This program demonstrates the use of the stat structure, and should make things much clearer.

Reading Directories

As mentioned previously, a directory is simply a special file that contains i-number/filename pairs. With the exception of 4.2 and 4.3BSD, all versions of the UNIX system limit filenames to 14 characters. These short filenames make for a simple directory format, so we'll look at a program to read directories on non-BSD systems first. A program to read the directories containing longer Berkeley-style filenames will be shown afterwards.

A directory contains structures of type direct, defined in the include file *sys/dir.h* (once again, *sys/types.h* must be included to define the types used in the structure):

```
#define DIRSIZ    14

struct direct {
    ino_t    d_ino;
    char     d_name[DIRSIZ];
};
```

It should be noted that the name of the file, d_name, is *not* guaranteed to be null-terminated; programs should always be careful of this. Files which have been deleted will have i-numbers (d_ino) equal to zero; these should in general be skipped over when reading the directory. A directory is read by simply opening it and reading structures either one at a time or all at once. Example 4-1 shows a small program that simply opens the current directory and prints the names of all the files it contains. (Remember, this program will only work on non-Berkeley UNIX systems.)

Example 4-1. listfiles1—list the names of the files in the current directory

```
/*
 * Non-BSD systems only.
 */
#include <sys/types.h>
#include <sys/dir.h>
#include <stdio.h>

main()
{
    FILE *fp;
    struct direct dir;

    if ((fp = fopen(".", "r")) == NULL) {
        perror("current directory");
        exit(1);
    }

    /*
     * Read directory entries.  Since we're reading
     * entries one at a time, we use the fread routine,
     * which buffers them internally.  Don't use the
     * low-level read to do things this way, since
     * reading very small quantities of data (16 bytes)
     * at a time is very inefficient.
     */
    while ((n = fread((char *)&dir, sizeof(dir), 1, fp) != EOF) {
        /*
         * Skip removed files.
```

```
        */
        if (dir.d_ino == 0)
            continue;
        /*
         * Make sure we print no more than DIRSIZ
         * characters.
         */
        printf("%.*s\n", DIRSIZ, dir.d_name);
    }

    fclose(fp);
    exit(0);
}
```

In 4.2BSD, the 14-character limit on filenames was removed and filenames were allowed to be much longer.* Obviously, storing directories in the same fixed-size format would be quite inefficient, since filenames are seldom extremely long. Instead, the directory entry is stored as a variable-length record, and a special set of library routines have been provided to read directories. Public-domain versions of these routines are available on most newer UNIX systems, and should always be used in order to write portable code. As an aid to portability, a listing of these routines is provided in Appendix D, *Berkeley UNIX Directory Compatibility Routines*, for use on older systems that do not already provide them.

Even with all these changes, the directory structure is still defined in *sys/dir.h* on Berkeley UNIX. The filename in this structure is always guaranteed to be null-terminated (which is not the case on non-Berkeley UNIX systems). To read a directory, the user declares a pointer of type DIR, similar to stdio's FILE pointer. The opendir routine opens the directory given as argument and returns a pointer of this type or NULL if the directory cannot be opened. The readdir routine returns a pointer to a directory entry, or NULL on end-of-file. The closedir routine closes the directory file. In addition, the seekdir and rewinddir routines are provided to change the current location and reset the location to zero in the directory. The scandir routine provides an alternative to reading the directory entries one at a time; it reads the entire directory into memory and sorts the entries using user-supplied selection and sorting routines. Example 4-2 shows the use of these routines to print the names of the files in the current directory.

Example 4-2. listfiles2—list the names of the files in the current directory

```
/*
 * For use with 4.2 and 4.3BSD systems.
 */
#include <sys/types.h>
```

---

*Usually, the limit is 256 characters.

```
#include <sys/dir.h>
#include <stdio.h>

main()
{
    DIR *dp;
    struct direct *dir;

    if ((dp = opendir(".")) == NULL) {
        fprintf(stderr, "cannot open directory.\n");
        exit(1);
    }

    /*
     * Read entries...
     */
    while ((dir = readdir(dp)) != NULL) {
        /*
         * Skip removed files.
         */
        if (dir->d_ino == 0)
            continue;

        printf("%s\n", dir->d_name);
    }

    closedir(dp);
    exit(0);
}
```

In order to consolidate the information provided in the preceding sections, Example 4-3 shows a program similar in function to the standard UNIX program *ls*. This program will perform an `ls -asl` on each of its named arguments. If the argument is a directory, the contents of that directory will be listed. For simplicity's sake the program prints the user id and group id of the owner of each file rather than digging up the login and group names. Also, the filenames are not sorted, and the directory is simply printed in the order it is read. The directory reading routines of Berkeley UNIX are used in the example; you should be able to change this yourself if necessary.

Example 4-3. ls—an "ls"-like program

```
#include <sys/types.h>
#include <sys/stat.h>
#include <sys/dir.h>
#include <stdio.h>

char *modes[] = {
    "---", "--x", "-w-", "-wx",
    "r--", "r-x", "rw-", "rwx"
};
```

```
main(argc, argv)
int argc;
char **argv;
{
    struct stat sbuf;

    /*
     * If no arguments, list current directory.
     */
    if (argc < 2) {
        list(".");
        exit(0);
    }

    /*
     * Process arguments.
     */
    while (--argc) {
        /*
         * See what the file is.
         */
        if (stat(*++argv, &sbuf) < 0) {
            perror(*argv);
            continue;
        }

        /*
         * If it's a directory we list it,
         * otherwise just print the info about
         * the file.
         */
        if ((sbuf.st_mode & S_IFMT) == S_IFDIR)
            list(*argv);
        else
            printout(".", *argv);
    }

    exit(0);
}

/*
 * list--read a directory and list the files it
 *          contains.
 */
list(name)
char *name;
{
    DIR *dp;
    struct direct *dir;

    /*
     * Open the directory.
     */
```

```
        if ((dp = opendir(name)) == NULL) {
            fprintf(stderr, "%s: cannot open.\n", name);
            return;
        }

        /*
         * For each entry...
         */
        while ((dir = readdir(dp)) != NULL) {
            /*
             * Skip removed files.
             */
            if (dir->d_ino == 0)
                continue;

            /*
             * Print it out.
             */
            printout(name, dir->d_name);
        }

        closedir(dp);
}
# define BLKSIZE 1024

/*
 * printout—print out the information about
 *              a file.
 */
printout(dir, name)
char *dir, *name;
{
        int i, j;
        char perms[10];
        struct stat sbuf;
        char newname[BLKSIZE];

        /*
         * Make full path name, so
         * we have a legal path.
         */
        sprintf(newname, "%s/%s", dir, name);

        /*
         * At this point we know the file exists,
         * so this won't fail.
         */
        stat(newname, &sbuf);

        /*
         * Print size in kbytes.
         */
        printf("%5d ", (sbuf.st_size + BLKSIZE-1) / BLKSIZE);
```

```
/*
 * Get the file type.  For convenience (and to
 * make this example universal), we ignore the
 * other types which are version-dependent.
 */
switch (sbuf.st_mode & S_IFMT) {
case S_IFREG:    putchar('-'); break;
case S_IFDIR:    putchar('d'); break;
case S_IFCHR:    putchar('c'); break;
case S_IFBLK:    putchar('b'); break;
default:         putchar('?'); break;
}


/*
 * Get each of the three groups of permissions
 * (owner, group, world).  Since they're just
 * bits, we can count in binary and use this
 * as a subscript (see the modes array, above).
 */
*perms = '\0';
for (i=2; i >= 0; i--) {
    /*
     * Since we're subscripting, we don't
     * need the constants.  Just get a
     * value between 0 and 7.
     */
    j = (sbuf.st_mode >> (i*3)) & 07;

    /*
     * Get the perm bits.
     */
    strcat(perms, modes[j]);
}

/*
 * Handle special bits which replace the 'x'
 * in places.
 */
if ((sbuf.st_mode & S_ISUID) != 0)
    perms[2] = 's';
if ((sbuf.st_mode & S_ISGID) != 0)
    perms[5] = 's';
if ((sbuf.st_mode & S_ISVTX) != 0)
    perms[8] = 't';

/*
 * Print permissions, number of links,
 * user and group ids.
 */
printf("%s%3d %5d/%-5d ", perms, sbuf.st_nlink, sbuf.st_uid,
    sbuf.st_gid);

/*
```

```
        * Print the size of the file in bytes,
        * and the last modification time.  The
        * ctime routine converts a time to ASCII;
        * it is described in Chapter 7, Telling
        * Time and Timing Things.
        */
       printf("%7d %.12s ", sbuf.st_size, ctime(&sbuf.st_mtime)+4);

       /*
        * Finally, print the filename.
        */
       printf("%s\n", name);
   }
```

Modifying File Attributes

The chmod system call is used to change the mode of a file. It takes two arguments: a character string containing the name of the file to change, and the new
mode to set given as an integer. A similar call, fchmod, which takes an open file
descriptor in place of a filename, is provided in Berkeley UNIX. The mode is conventionally specified in octal, which lets each digit represent one group of permissions (owner, group, world). The calls return −1 and set the errno variable
if the file does not exist or is not owned by the user running the program, or 0 on
success.

The chown system call is used to change file ownership. It takes three arguments: a character string containing the name of the file to be changed, an integer
containing the new user id to set, and an integer containing the new group id to
set. Berkeley UNIX also provides the call fchown, which takes an open file
descriptor in place of the filename. This call is normally restricted to the super-
user. It returns 0 on success; −1 is returned and errno is set if the call fails.

Miscellaneous File System Routines

The rest of this chapter is devoted to the "little" routines that don't fit into their
own section but are nevertheless important.

Changing Directories

A program can change its current working directory with the chdir system call. It takes a single argument, the path name of the new directory. −1 is returned if the program cannot change into the directory, and errno is set to the reason for failure.

Berkeley UNIX and System V each provide routines to obtain the path names of the current working directory; these are discussed in Chapter 13, *Miscellaneous Routines*.

Deleting and Truncating Files

Files can be deleted using the unlink system call. It takes a single argument, the name of the file to be deleted. −1 is returned if the file cannot be removed, and errno is set to the error condition. To remove a file, the user running the program must be able to write in the directory containing the file. He does *not* need write permission on the file itself.

unlink will not delete directories. To remove a directory on UNIX systems prior to 4.2BSD and System V Release 3.0, the rmdir system program must be executed;* there is no system call to perform this function. In 4.2BSD, rmdir was turned into a system call taking a single argument, the name of the directory to be removed. −1 is returned if an error occurs, and errno will be set to the reason for failure. The rmdir system call was added to System V in Release 3.0, and is called the same way. Note that only empty directories may be removed.

In Berkeley UNIX, the truncate system call may be used to truncate a file to a given size. The call takes two arguments: the name of the file to be truncated and the number of bytes the file should be truncated to. If the file is already smaller than the specified number of bytes, nothing is done (it is not extended to that size). An alternate form of the call, ftruncate, which takes an open file descriptor in place of the filename, is also available.

Making Directories

On UNIX systems prior to 4.2BSD and System V Release 3.0, the mkdir system program must be executed to create a directory. In 4.2BSD, mkdir was turned into a system call. It takes two arguments: the name of the directory to be

---

*See Chapter 9, *Executing Programs*.

created, and the mode the directory should be given. −1 is returned on error, and `errno` will be set to the reason for failure. The `mkdir` system call was added to System V in Release 3.0, and is called in the same fashion.

Linking and Renaming Files

To make a hard link to a file, the `link` system call is used. This call takes two arguments: the name of the file to be linked to, and the name of the link to be created. −1 is returned if the link cannot be made, and `errno` is set to the error condition. It is not possible to make links across mounted file systems.

To rename a file on non-Berkeley systems, a series of `link` and `unlink` calls are used, as follows:

```
unlink(newfile);
link(oldfile, newfile);
unlink(oldfile);
```

This only works if the old and new files are in the same file system; cross-file system moves must be done by copying the file in place of linking. Directories may be linked, but they must be empty; the user doing the linking must have super-user privileges. In general, directories should be linked using symbolic links, not hard links.

To rename a file under Berkeley UNIX, the `rename` system call should be used instead. `rename` guarantees that one instance of the file will always exist, even if the system crashes in the middle of the operation. It takes two arguments: the name of the file to be moved, and the name it should be moved to. As above, this only works on moves that do not cross file system boundaries.

Symbolic Links

In 4.2BSD, symbolic links were added to the file system. These links are simply "pointers" to files; they are not hard links. Unlike hard links, they may cross file system boundaries. To create a symbolic link, the `symlink` call is used. It takes two arguments: the name of the file to be pointed to, and the name of the link itself. −1 is returned and `errno` is set on error.

To find out what a symbolic link points to, the `readlink` system call is used. This call takes three arguments: the name of the link, a pointer to a character buffer to store the name of the pointed-to file in, and the size of the buffer. The number of bytes placed in the buffer is returned on success; this number is important because the buffer is not null-terminated. −1 is returned if the call fails and `errno` is set to the error condition.

It should be noted that access permissions are ignored on symbolic links; even a mode 0 (l---------) symbolic link can be used by anyone, and can be read by anyone using readlink. This is to avoid the problem of differing modes on the symbolic link and the file it points to.

The umask Value

When a file is created with creat or the three-argument open, a mode is supplied for the file to be created with. Invisibly to you, this mode is *modified* by the program's *umask*. The umask is a number just like the mode, except it indicates permissions to be turned *off* rather than on. For example, if the program's umask is 0022 and a file is created mode 0666, the actual mode of the file will be computed as:

```
file_mode = create_mode & ~umask;
```

so the actual mode of this file will be:

```
0666 & ~0022 = 0666 & 0755 = 0644
```

The umask value only affects creation modes of files and directories; the modes supplied to the chmod call are not affected.

Most systems have a default umask value of 0 or 022. The umask may be changed with the umask system call, which takes the new value as an argument and returns the old value.

5

Device I/O Control

The Version 7 and Berkeley UNIX ioctl
The System V ioctl
The fcntl System Call
Non-blocking I/O
The select System Call

Controlling input and output devices is an important topic for several reasons. Some examples include:

- When prompting for a password, it is normally desirable to prevent the computer from echoing (printing) the characters typed and thus giving the password away.

- Many people like to adjust various input control characters on their terminal, such as the "erase," "kill," and "interrupt" characters.

- Programs accessing the magnetic tape device often need to rewind the tape, skip over files on the tape, take the tape drive off-line, etc.

All versions of the UNIX operating system provide one "catch-all" system call for controlling input and output at the device level. This call is ioctl. It takes three arguments: an open file descriptor referring to the device or file in question,* a constant representing the operation to be performed, and an argument for

---

*Depending on the operation being performed, the file descriptor may be required to be open for reading and/or writing. It is usually safe to assume that a file descriptor open for writing will be accepted.

the operation to use. The argument is often given as a pointer to something; depending on the operation "something" is either a structure or a long integer.

Version 7 and the Berkeley versions of UNIX use the same operation constants and third arguments, and code is generally portable between these versions (although several features added by Berkeley will not be available on Version 7 systems). In System V, on the other hand, AT&T has completely redone the operations and their arguments. The purpose of this was to make everything work the same way, and to centralize many functions. Unfortunately, this means that code using ioctl will not be portable between System V and any other version of UNIX, and vice-versa.

Two other calls often used in older versions of UNIX for controlling terminal modes are gtty (get tty modes) and stty (set tty modes). These are not available at all in System V; they are provided as compatibility library routines in Berkeley UNIX. Their function is duplicated exactly by the TIOCGETP and TIOCSETP ioctl operations; they will not be discussed further. Another system call, fcntl, was added in System V and 4.2BSD to attempt to remove the file operations from ioctl. This call is discussed following the sections on ioctl.

Discussion of the ioctl system call has been divided into two main parts: the first describes the Version 7/Berkeley UNIX version, the second describes the System V version. For simplicity, only terminal I/O control will be described. Once the basic concepts are understood, they may easily be extended to other devices.

The Version 7 and Berkeley UNIX ioctl

Version 7 and Berkeley versions of UNIX have two structures available for modifying terminal modes. The Berkeley versions also have a third structure and a 32-bit word for controlling the added features in their terminal driver. These structures are described in the following sections, along with the various operation codes which use them.

The definitions of the structures and the operations are contained in the include file *sys/ioctl.h* ; *sys/types.h* should also be included.* For all operations, ioctl returns 0 if the call succeeds. If it fails, −1 is returned and errno is set to the error condition.

---

*On some older systems it may be necessary to include *sgtty.h* as well as the other files; newer systems permit inclusion of either file (the files include each other).

Line Disciplines

In Berkeley UNIX, many features such as job control, etc. have been incorporated into a second version of the terminal (tty) driver. The original tty driver, which is basically identical to the Version 7 driver, is called the "old" tty driver while the new version is called (obviously) the "new" tty driver. It is possible to choose among several *line disciplines* to use when communicating over serial lines; the tty drivers are two of these disciplines.

To determine which line discipline is currently in use, the call:

```
ioctl(fd, TIOCGETD, &ldisc)
```

should be used, where `fd` is an open file descriptor referring to a serial line (e.g., a terminal), and `ldisc` is a long integer. Following the call, the value of `ldisc` may be compared against the constants:

OTTYDISC   The "old" tty discipline. This discipline is more or less identical to the Version 7 tty driver.

NTTYDISC   The "new" tty discipline. This discipline has everything the old discipline has, and also supports job control, command line redraw, etc.

NETLDISC   The Berknet line discipline. This is essentially obsolete as of 4.2BSD, but is still around. (Berknet was a set of protocols for joining several machines together into a primitive network using serial data lines. The software provided facilities for file transfer and remote job execution. Berknet was superseded by TCP/IP (see Chapter 12, *Networking*), which is both faster and more robust.)

There are several other disciplines available, but they vary from site to site and version to version. To set the line discipline, the call:

```
ioctl(fd, TIOCSETD, &ldisc)
```

should be used. In this case, `ldisc` should contain the value associated with the desired new discipline.

In the following discussion, it may be assumed that anything which works with the old tty driver will work on both Version 7 and Berkeley UNIX systems. Further, unless the new tty driver implements the function differently (line kill, for example), all old tty driver operations work equally well on the new tty driver. Those functions described as only working with the new tty driver will only work on Berkeley UNIX systems, and only if the line discipline is set to NTTYDISC.

The sgttyb Structure

The sgttyb structure is used by both the old and new tty drivers to set the input and output baud rates, the erase and line kill characters, and many of the more often used terminal modes. The structure is defined as follows:

```
struct sgttyb {
    char    sg_ispeed;    /* input speed    */
    char    sg_ospeed;    /* output speed   */
    char    sg_erase;     /* erase character */
    char    sg_kill;      /* kill character */
    short   sg_flags;     /* mode flags     */
};
```

sg_ispeed and sg_ospeed have values from the set of constants B0, B50, B75, B110, B134, B150, B200, B300, B600, B1200, B1800, B2400, B4800, B9600. The sg_flags word has 16 bits which represent various modes. If the bit is set the mode is on, otherwise it is off. The operations using this structure are:

TIOCGETP   Get the current modes.

TIOCSETP   Set the modes to those in the structure pointed to by the third argument. Note that all elements must be ''filled in''; the easiest way to do this is to use TIOCGETP to get the current modes, modify that structure, and then set the new modes.

TIOCSETN   The same as TIOCSETP, except that the input and output queues are not flushed when the request is performed. This version is necessary to keep output from disappearing, which is often desired.

The sg_flags word is used to set various modes; the full set of them is described in *tty* (4). Some of the more common (and interesting) ones are:

ECHO   When set, the operating system will print to the terminal screen all characters typed on the terminal keyboard. When not set, nothing is printed and the cursor does not move. This is useful for prompting for passwords, etc.

RAW   When set, *all* input processing is disabled. This means that characters may have their eighth bit set (which can confuse stdio routines, since the negative character can get sign-extended into –1). In addition, input is not buffered; all reads from the terminal will return as soon as a character is typed rather than waiting until a carriage return is typed. In RAW mode, all special characters (erase, kill, interrupt, etc.) lose their special meanings and will not perform those functions.

CBREAK   When set, *some* of the input processing is turned off. Characters are still returned as 7-bit ASCII (eighth bit is zero), and the interrupt character still works. The erase and kill characters are disabled, and reads still return as soon as a character is typed. In general it is usually preferable to use CBREAK over RAW, since the interface is somewhat cleaner.

CRMOD   If not set, the system will accept either carriage return or line feed as a command line terminator. It will map the carriage return into a line feed character for the reading process, and will echo a carriage return and a line feed on output. If set, this mapping is disabled, and a carriage return will simply be sent to the reading process as is, and the system will only echo the character typed instead of mapping one into the other.

The conventional way to turn on a mode is to OR the constant for that mode into the flags word. To turn off a mode the *complement* of the constant for that mode is ANDed with the flags word. For example, to turn ECHO on and RAW off, the code segment:

```
flags |= ECHO;
flags &= ~RAW;
```

might be used. A complete example is given later in Example 5-1.

The tchars Structure

The tchars structure is used by both the old and new tty drivers to set the interrupt, quit, start, stop, and end of file characters. The structure is defined as:

```
struct tchars {
     char    t_intrc;     /* interrupt     */
     char    t_quitc;     /* quit          */
     char    t_startc;    /* start output  */
     char    t_stopc;     /* stop output   */
     char    t_eofc;      /* end-of-file   */
     char    t_brkc;      /* input delimiter */
};
```

The associated operation constants are:

TIOCGETC   Get the current settings.

TIOCSETC   Set new characters. Note that all elements of the structure should be filled in.

By setting any of the elements of the structure to −1, that character is effectively undefined until it is reset to something else. This is one way of making a process uninterruptible from the keyboard. This convention of setting things to –1 is also true for the sgttyb and ltchars structures.

The ltchars Structure

The ltchars structure is used by the new tty driver to set the extra control characters for suspend, delayed suspend, reprint command line, flush output, erase word, and quote next character. The structure is defined as:

```
struct ltchars {
    char    t_suspc;        /* stop process signal    */
    char    t_dsuspc;       /* delayed stop process   */
    char    t_rprntc;       /* reprint line           */
    char    t_flushc;       /* flush output (toggle)  */
    char    t_werasc;       /* word erase             */
    char    t_lnextc;       /* literal next char      */
};
```

The associated operation constants are:

TIOCGLTC   Get the current settings.

TIOCSLTC   Set new characters. Note that all elements of the structure should be filled in.

The Local Mode Word

The additional modes available in the new tty driver* are set in the *local mode word*. This word is similar in function to the sg_flags word in the sgttyb structure, and is simply a 32-bit integer passed to ioctl with one of the operation constants discussed below.

Some of the more useful modes are:

LCRTBS   Perform a backspace when the erase character is typed, instead of erasing the character.

LCRTERA   Perform backspacing for CRT terminals by printing "backspace space backspace" for each character, thus erasing it on the screen.

LCRTKIL   Perform line kills by erasing the entire line using the "backspace space backspace" method. This is different from the old tty driver; which simply echoes a new line.

---

*In Berkeley UNIX, many of these modes have been back-ported to the old tty driver, although this is not documented anywhere.

LCTLECH   Print input control characters (except the erase and kill characters) as ^X, where *X* is the control character. Normally, the character is just echoed as is (e.g., ^G, the bell character, beeps).

LTOSTOP   When this mode is set, and a background process tries to write to the terminal, it is stopped via a signal* and cannot write to the terminal until it is placed in the foreground. This is relatively useless unless the user is using *csh* or another shell that understands job control.

The associated operation constants are:

TIOCLGET   Get the current mode word.

TIOCLSET   Set the mode word to the new value.

TIOCLBIS   Set the '1' bits of the argument in the mode word. The argument is ORed with the current value of the mode word and the result stored in the mode word.

TIOCLBIC   Clear the '1' bits of the argument in the mode word. The complement of the argument is ANDed with the current value of the mode word and the result stored in the mode word.

The winsize Structure

In 4.3BSD, support for windowing systems such as SunView®, the X Window System, and the software for the Teletype 5620 terminal was added to the terminal driver. This includes a new structure which defines the size of a window. Programs such as *vi* and *more* use the information about window size to determine the number of rows and columns on the ''screen.'' The structure is defined as:

```
struct winsize {
    unsigned short    ws_row;      /* character size */
    unsigned short    ws_col;
    unsigned short    ws_xpixel;   /* pixel size     */
    unsigned short    ws_ypixel;
};
```

The associated operation codes are TIOCGWINSZ to get the current window size, and TIOCSWINSZ to set a new window size. When getting the window size, if either ws_row or ws_col is zero in the returned structure, the entire structure should be ignored, as no window size has been set (i.e., the terminal is probably not running a window package).

---

*See Chapter 10, *Job Control.*

When a window's size is changed, either by you (using a mouse or other device) or by a program, all programs in the terminal's process group are sent the SIGWINCH signal indicating a size change.* This enables editors and the like to re-format the screen according to the new size.

Miscellaneous Operations

The following operation constants are also available. There are several more, but they are rather special-purpose and not described here.

TIOCFLUSH Flush all characters remaining in the input and output queues. This is primarily useful for discarding any "typeahead" the user may have entered.

TIOCEXCL Set exclusive-use on the file referred to by the file descriptor. This file does not have to be a terminal. When exclusive-use is set, all opens of that file will be denied until the current process closes the file.

TIOCNXCL Clear exclusive-use on the file referred to by the file descriptor. This should always be used by processes setting exclusive-use before they exit.

TIOCSTI Put the character pointed to by the third argument onto the input queue of the terminal referred to by the file descriptor. This effectively "pretends" that the user typed this character. Because this is a potential security hole, there are several restrictions (which vary from site to site) on its use.

FIONREAD The number of characters available to read from the file descriptor is returned in the third argument. This is useful for determining if the user has typed something without executing a read (which would "block" waiting for him to type something if he hadn't already).

Example 5-1 shows a small program that turns off ECHO and turns on CBREAK, and then prints screenfuls of the files named on its command line. The program pauses after each screenful and waits for you to type any character to continue. Because the terminal is in CBREAK mode, the read will return immediately. When all files have been displayed, the program resets the terminal modes and exits. This is a primitive version of the Berkeley UNIX *more* and System V *pg* commands. Note that the tchars structure is used to "turn off" the interrupt character while the program is in use; this prevents you from interrupting out of the program and leaving the terminal in an undesirable state.†

---

*See Chapter 8, *Processing Signals*, and Chapter 10, *Job Control*.
†This is *not* the way it is done in real life; see Chapter 8, *Processing Signals*.

Example 5-1. pager1—simple file paginator (Berkeley/V7 systems)

```
#include <sys/ioctl.h>
#include <stdio.h>

main(argc, argv)
int argc;
char **argv;
{
    struct sgttyb sgo, sgn;
    struct tchars tco, tcn;

    if (argc < 2) {
        fprintf(stderr, "Usage: %s file [file ...]\n", *argv);
        exit(1);
    }

    /*
     * In real life we'd check the return values of
     * these, since if the input is redirected from
     * a file they will fail.  We are assuming the
     * terminal is always connected to the standard
     * input.
     */
    ioctl(0, TIOCGETP, &sgo);
    ioctl(0, TIOCGETC, &tco);

    sgn = sgo;
    sgn.sg_flags &= ~ECHO;       /* turn off ECHO   */
    sgn.sg_flags |= CBREAK;      /* turn on CBREAK  */

    tcn = tco;
    tcn.t_intrc = -1;            /* disable int key */

    /*
     * Set the new modes.  Again we ignore return
     * values.
     */
    ioctl(0, TIOCSETP, &sgn);
    ioctl(0, TIOCSETC, &tcn);

    while (--argc)
        more(*++argv);

    /*
     * Reset the old tty modes.
     */
    ioctl(0, TIOCSETP, &sgo);
    ioctl(0, TIOCSETC, &tco);

    exit(0);
}
```

```
/*
 * more—display the file.
 */
more(file)
char *file;
{
    FILE *fp;
    int line;
    char linebuf[1024];

    if ((fp = fopen(file, "r")) == NULL) {
        perror(file);
        return;
    }

    /*
     * Print 22 lines at a time.
     */
    for (;;) {
        line = 1;
        while (line < 22) {
            /*
             * If end-of-file, let them hit a key one
             * more time and then go back.
             */
            if (fgets(linebuf, sizeof(linebuf), fp) == NULL) {
                fclose(fp);
                prompt();
                return;
            }

            fwrite(linebuf, 1, strlen(linebuf), stdout);
            line++;
        }

        prompt();
    }
}

/*
 * prompt—prompt for a character.
 */
prompt()
{
    int answer;

    printf("Type any character for next page: ");
    answer = getchar();
    putchar('\n');
}
```

There are many, many more things which may be done with the `ioctl` system call, including magnetic tape manipulation, network routing changes, etc. All of the operations are described in the various manual pages contained in Section 4 of the *UNIX Programmer's Manual*. The operations described here are all documented in *tty* (4).

The System V ioctl

The System V version of `ioctl` is completely incompatible with the `ioctl` supplied with most other versions of UNIX. It uses a single structure for all operations; this structure is defined in the include file *termio.h* :

```
#define NCC      8

struct termio {
    unsigned short c_iflag;      /* input modes    */
    unsigned short c_oflag;      /* output modes   */
    unsigned short c_cflag;      /* control modes  */
    unsigned short c_lflag;      /* local modes    */
    char           c_line;       /* line discipline */
    unsigned char  c_cc[NCC];    /* control chars  */
};
```

The associated `ioctl` operation constants are:

TCGETA   Get the current settings.

TCSETA   Set the new modes from the structure pointed to by the argument.

TCSETAW   Wait for output to drain before setting the new modes. This is often needed at low baud rates to prevent disappearing output.

TCSETAF   Wait for the output to drain, and then flush the input queue and set the new modes.

Each element of the structure is described separately below.

c_iflag

This field describes the basic terminal input control. There are several flags that can be set and cleared in this field. Unlike Version 7 and Berkeley UNIX flags words, System V often uses two separate bits to indicate the "on" and "off" of a single feature. The code naively assumes that you will not set both the "on" and "off" flags; results in this case are undefined.

The conventional way to turn on a mode is to OR the constant for that mode into the flags word. To turn off a mode the *complement* of the constant for that mode is ANDed with the flags word. For example, to turn ISTRIP on and IGNCR off, the code segment:

```
flags |= ISTRIP;
flags &= ~IGNCR;
```

might be used. A complete example is given later in Example 5-2.

Some of the more important bits for c_iflag are:

BRKINT   If set, then the BREAK key will generate an interrupt signal just as (conventionally) the DEL key does.

IGNBRK   The inverse of BRKINT.

ISTRIP   Strip (set to zero) the eighth bit off all input characters. If not set, the eighth bit is passed through exactly as received.

INLCR   If set, line feed is mapped to carriage return on input.

ICRNL   If set, carriage return is mapped to line feed on input.

IGNCR   If set, carriage return is ignored on input.

IXON   Enables start/stop (usually ^S/^Q) output flow control. All start/stop characters are ignored with respect to actually passing them to a program. If IXANY is set, then any character will restart the output, otherwise only ^Q will restart it.

c_oflag

This field specifies the system's treatment of output. Some of the more important bits are:

OPOST   If set, the rest of the flags in this field take effect. If not set, all output it passed straight through to the terminal; this set of modes will be ignored.

ONLCR   Map line feed to carriage return-line feed on output.

OCRNL   Map carriage return to line feed on output.

c_cflag

This field describes the hardware control of the terminal. This is where baud rate, parity, etc. are all set. There are constants for all these features defined; see the include file or the *termio*(7) manual page for their values.

c_lflag

This field is used by the line discipline to control terminal functions. Some of the modes provided are:

ISIG   If set, the INTR, SWTCH, and QUIT (see below) characters have their normal meanings and cause interrupts to be generated. If not set, these characters have no special meaning.

ICANON   If set, canonical input processing is enabled. This means that characters are buffered until a carriage return (line feed) is typed, and the character erase and line kill functions work as normal. If not set, then read requests return "immediately" with single characters. Actually, values for *min* and *time* should be placed in the VMIN and VTIME elements of the c_cc array when turning off ICANON. A read will not be satisfied until at least *min* characters have been received or the timeout value *time* (in tenths of seconds) has been reached between characters. To emulate the Version 7 and Berkeley UNIX RAW or CBREAK modes, *min* should be 1 and *time* should be 0.

ECHO   If set, characters are printed as they are typed. If not set, nothing is printed. This is useful for prompting for passwords and the like.

ECHOE   If set, character erase is echoed as "backspace space backspace."

ECHOK   If set, a line feed is echoed after a kill character is typed.

c_cc

This array holds the values of the various special characters. It is subscripted with the constants VINTR, VQUIT, VERASE, VKILL, VEOF, VEOL, and VSWTCH, which should have the obvious meanings. The VSWTCH character is for System V's layer-based job control facility. The start and stop characters *may not be changed* and *may not be disabled*. All the other characters may be changed or disabled (by setting them to –1) at will. This problem with the start and stop characters causes problems for several programs such as text editors.

Example 5-2 shows a small program that turns off ECHO and ICANON, and then prints screenfuls of the files named on its command line. The program pauses after each screenful and waits for you to type any character to continue. Because the terminal is not in ICANON mode, the read will return immediately. When all files have been displayed, the program resets the terminal modes and exits. Again, this is a primitive version of the Berkeley UNIX *more* and System V *pg* commands. Note that the interrupt character in c_cc is set to –1 to "turn it off" while the program is in use; this prevents you from interrupting out of the program and leaving the terminal in an undesirable state.*

---

*This is *not* the way it is done in real life; see Chapter 8, *Processing Signals*.

Example 5-2. pager2—simple file paginator (System V version)

```c
#include <termio.h>
#include <stdio.h>

main(argc, argv)
int argc;
char **argv;
{
    struct termio tio, tin;

    if (argc < 2) {
        fprintf(stderr, "Usage: %s file [file ...]\n", *argv);
        exit(1);
    }

    /*
     * In real life we'd check the return value of
     * this, since if the input is redirected from a
     * file it will fail.  We are assuming the
     * terminal is always connected to the standard
     * input.
     */
    ioctl(0, TCGETA, &tio);

    tin = tio;
    tin.c_lflag &= ~ECHO;       /* turn off ECHO   */
    tin.c_lflag &= ~ICANON;     /* turn off ICANON */

    /*
     * Emulate CBREAK mode.
     */
    tin.c_cc[VMIN] = 1;
    tin.c_cc[VTIME] = 0;

    /*
     * Set the new modes.  Again we ignore return
     * values.
     */
    ioctl(0, TCSETA, &tin);

    while (--argc)
        more(*++argv);

    /*
     * Reset the old tty modes.
     */
    ioctl(0, TCSETA, &tio);

    exit(0);
}

/*
```

```
 * more—display the file.
 */
more(file)
char *file;
{
    FILE *fp;
    int line;
    char linebuf[1024];

    if ((fp = fopen(file, "r")) == NULL) {
        perror(file);
        return;
    }

    /*
     * Print 22 lines at a time.
     */
    for (;;) {
        line = 1;
        while (line < 22) {
            /*
             * If end-of-file, let them hit a key one
             * more time and then go back.
             */
            if (fgets(linebuf, sizeof(linebuf), fp) == NULL) {
                fclose(fp);
                prompt();
                return;
            }

            fwrite(linebuf, 1, strlen(linebuf), stdout);
            line++;
        }

        prompt();
    }
}

/*
 * prompt—prompt for a character.
 */
prompt()
{
    int answer;

    printf("Type any character for next page: ");
    answer = getchar();
    putchar('\n');
}
```

There are a few more options available in the System V ioctl not described here, but they are fairly special-purpose. The material described in this section is fully covered in the System V manual in Section 7.

The fcntl System Call

In UNIX System V, the fcntl system call was added to the system to handle file control operations. This call replaced the dup2 system call, as well as handling other operations. In 4.2BSD, fcntl was added to be compatible with System V. Unfortunately, the two versions of the call are only partially compatible. The System V version provides functions that the Berkeley one does not (file locking), and the Berkeley version provides functions that the System V one does not (asynchronous I/O through the use of signals). For this reason, the call will only be discussed in a general sense here.

fcntl takes three arguments: a file descriptor referring to an open file (*fd*), a constant indicating the requested operation, and an integer argument used for various purposes (*arg*). It returns any of several values depending on the operation requested, but if the call fails, −1 is always returned and errno is set to the error which occurred. The operation constants are defined in the include file *fcntl.h* , and are very briefly described below. Some of the concepts mentioned below will be described in later chapters; also see the documentation on fcntl in Section 2 of *The UNIX Programmer's Manual* .

F_DUPFD   Provide a duplicate file descriptor; this replaces dup2 on System V.

F_GETFD   Get the file's close-on-exec flag. 0 in the low-order bit means the file will stay open, 1 means it will be closed.*

F_SETFD   Set the file's close-on-exec flag to arg.

F_GETFL   Get file status flags. The flags are described in fcntl(2).

F_SETFL   Set file status flags to arg. The flags are described in fcntl(2).

F_GETOWN   Get process group to receive SIGIO and SIGURG signals about fd (Berkeley UNIX only).†

F_SETOWN   Set process group to receive SIGIO and SIGURG signals about fd to arg (Berkeley UNIX only).

F_GETLK   Get first lock on file which blocks type described in the *flock*-type structure pointed to by arg (System V only).

---

*See Chapter 9, *Executing Programs*.
†See Chapter 8, *Processing Signals*.

F_SETLK   Set or clear a file segment lock according to *flock* -type structure pointed to by arg (System V only).

F_SETLKW   A blocking version of F_SETLK (System V only).

The System V version of the operating system has no equivalent to the F_GETOWN and F_SETOWN feature.

Non-blocking I/O

Normally, when a process issues a read, that process is *blocked* until there is something to read. That is, the process essentially goes to sleep until the read returns either the data read in, end-of-file, or an error. This is not always desirable, however. By using either the F_SETFL operation of fcntl, or in Berkeley versions of UNIX the FIONBIO ioctl operation, it is possible to make reads (and other operations on the file descriptor) return an error immediately if the operation would block.* If this occurs, errno is set to EWOULDBLOCK.

This is not a terribly clean way of doing things. It usually provides several unexpected problems that the programmer must deal with. In 4.2BSD the need for non-blocking I/O was not entirely eliminated, but the select system call was added to the system. This system call provides a much cleaner way of doing several things that used to require the use of non-blocking I/O.

The select System Call

The select system call is used to perform I/O *multiplexing*—that is, it enables the programmer to manage reading and writing to several file descriptors at once without "blocking" indefinitely on any of the operations. select is used by the programmer to check the status of his open file descriptors before operating on them. For example, if the program continuously prints information to the screen, but should also process any input the user types, the program can use select to *poll* the terminal, and when characters are present to be read, it can read them in and process them.

select takes five arguments: nfds, an integer which indicates the number of file descriptors to be checked, readfds, writefds, and exceptfds, which are pointers to *file descriptor sets* indicating which file descriptors are to be

---

*In System V, passing the O_NDELAY option to open will also set non-blocking I/O. In Berkeley UNIX, this flag will cause the open not to block, but any I/O performed on the file will still block.

checked to see if they are ready for reading, ready for writing, or have some exceptional condition pending, respectively, and t imeout, a pointer to a structure of type t imeval. The first nfds descriptors are checked in each set (i.e., descriptors 0 through nfds−1). On return, select replaces the given descriptor sets with subsets consisting of those descriptors that are ready for the requested operation.

In 4.2BSD, file descriptor sets were represented by long integers (32 bits). File descriptor *i* was to be checked if the *i*th bit of the integer was equal to one. Thus, to set readfds to check the file descriptors fd1 and fd2, the code segment:

```
long readfds;

readfds = 0;
readfds |= (1 << fd1);
readfds |= (1 << fd2);
```

would be used. In 4.3BSD, a special data type, fd_set, was defined in *sys/types.h* . This data type is able to handle more than 32 file descriptors. In addition, special macros were defined to manipulate this data type: FD_ZERO(&*fdset*) initializes a descriptor set *fdset* to the null set. FD_SET(*fd,* &*fdset*) adds the file descriptor *fd* to the set *fdset*, while FD_CLR(*fd,* &*fdset*) removes *fd* from the set *fdset*. FD_ISSET(*fd,* &*fdset*) is nonzero if *fd* is a member of set *fdset*, zero otherwise.

If t imeout is a non-null pointer, it specifies the maximum amount of time to wait for the select operation to complete. If it is a null pointer, the select will block indefinitely (i.e., it won't return until one of the file descriptors being asked about is ready for whatever operation is being checked). In order to effect a poll, t imeval should point to a zero-valued t imeval structure.

Any of readfds, writefds, and except fds may be given as null pointers if no descriptors are of interest.

select returns the number of ready descriptors that are contained in all the descriptor sets, or −1 on failure (errno will contain the reason for failure). If the time limit expires, then select returns 0.

Example 5-3 shows a program which waits 15 seconds for the user to type something. If nothing is typed, the program will assume a default response. An alternative way to perform this function without using select is discussed in Chapter 8, *Processing Signals.*

Example 5-3. select—program to demonstrate the select system call

```
#include <sys/types.h>
#include <sys/time.h>
#include <stdio.h>

main()
{
    int n, nfds;
    char buf[32];
    fd_set readfds;
    struct timeval tv;

    /*
     * We will be reading from standard input (file
     * descriptor 0), so we want to know when the
     * user has typed something.
     */
    FD_ZERO(&readfds);
    FD_SET(0, &readfds);

    /*
     * Set the timeout for 15 seconds.
     */
    tv.tv_sec = 15;
    tv.tv_usec = 0;

    /*
     * Prompt for input.
     */
    printf("Type a word; if you don't in 15 ");
    printf("seconds I'll use \"WORD\": ");
    fflush(stdout);

    /*
     * Now call select.  We pass NULL for
     * writefds and exceptfds, since we
     * aren't interested in them.
     */
    nfds = select(1, &readfds, NULL, NULL, &tv);

    /*
     * Now we check the results.  If nfds is zero,
     * then we timed out, and should assume the
     * default.  Otherwise, if file descriptor 0
     * is set in readfds, that means that it is
     * ready to be read, and we can read something
     * from it.
     */
    if (nfds == 0) {
        strcpy(buf, "WORD");
    }
    else {
```

```
        if (FD_ISSET(0, &readfds)) {
            n = read(0, buf, sizeof(buf));
            buf[n>0? n-1: 0] = '\0';
        }
    }

    printf("\nThe word is: %s\n", buf);
    exit(0);
}
```

6

Information About Users

The Login Name
The User Id
The Group Id
Reading the Password File
Reading the Group File
Reading the utmp File

Several pieces of information are maintained about each user of the system. Most of this information is stored in the password file, */etc/passwd* , and the group file, */etc/group* . This chapter describes each piece of information, what the operating system uses it for, and how programs can access and change it.

The Login Name

Each user of the system is given a unique *login name*. This name consists of up to eight characters; usually only lower-case alphabetics and numerics are permitted. A user uses his login name to identify himself to the system when logging in. Login names are also used when sending electronic mail, to label output printed on the line printer, etc. The operating system kernel does not use the login name for anything; it is only used by user-level programs.

To obtain the login name of the user executing a program, the program may use the `getlogin` routine. This routine returns a pointer to a character string containing the user's login name, or NULL on failure. It should be noted that getlogin obtains the login name by searching */etc/utmp* for the terminal it is running on, and returning the login name logged in on that terminal. This method is often prone to error, for example, if the user executing the program has logged off, or if he has changed his effective user id (see below). System V provides the cuserid function in place of getlogin, which is much less error-prone. Another method of obtaining the login name, searching the environment, is described in Chapter 14, *Miscellaneous Routines*.

The User Id

Each process in the system has associated with it two integer numbers called the *real user id* and the *effective user id*. These numbers are used by the operating system kernel to determine the process's access permissions, record accounting information, etc. The real user id always identifies the user executing the process. Only the super-user may change his real user id, thus becoming another user. The effective user id is used to determine the process's permissions. Normally, the effective user id is equal to the real user id. By changing its effective user id, a process gains the permissions associated with the new user id (and, at least temporarily, loses those associated with its real user id).* A user id is always unique, and refers to only one user of the system.

A program uses the getuid and geteuid system calls to obtain its real and effective user ids, respectively. Both calls simply return the associated id as an integer; no errors can occur.

The real and effective user ids are changed using the setuid system call. This call takes a single argument, the new user id to be used. −1 is returned on error, and errno is set to the reason for failure. The real and effective user ids are set according to the following rules:

- If the effective user id of the calling process is super-user, the real user id and effective user id are set to the new user id. This permits the super-user to permanently change his identity.

- If the effective user id of the calling process is not super-user, but its real user id is equal to the new value, the effective user id is set to the new value. This permits a process to regain the permissions of the user executing it after application of the third rule, below.

---

*This change is usually invisible to users, and is used by system programs like the printer or mailer software to temporarily gain permissions a normal user does not have.

- If the effective user id of the calling process is not super-user, but the saved set-user-id of the process is equal to the new value, the effective user id is set to the new value. This permits a process to temporarily execute with the permissions of a user other than the one executing the program. The program may regain its original permissions using the second rule, above.

It is important to note that executing a set-user-id program does not automatically give the program the permissions of the user owning the program; the program itself must request these permissions.

In 4.2BSD, the setuid call was replaced by setreuid. This call takes two arguments, the desired real and effective user ids to be set. If either argument is equal to –1, that value will not be changed. In order to maintain backward compatibility, setuid is provided as a library routine. It is easily implemented as:

```
setuid(uid)
int uid;
{
    return(setreuid(uid, uid));
}
```

The Group Id

In addition to the real and effective user ids, the operating system associates a *real group id* and an *effective group id* with each process. These numbers are entirely analogous to the real and effective user ids, with the exception that they do not uniquely identify a specific user. Instead, several users may be members of the same group, permitting them to have access to files owned by that group while denying others access.

To obtain its real and effective group ids, a program may use the getgid and getegid system calls respectively. The real and effective group ids may be set using setgid; this call is entirely analogous to setuid, including the rules used to determine which id to set. As with setuid, setgid was replaced in 4.2BSD with the setregid call.

The Berkeley UNIX Group Mechanism

In Version 7, System V, and Berkeley versions prior to 4.2BSD, a user could be a member of only one group at a time. In order to change groups, he was required to execute the newgrp command, which would change his group id and execute a new shell. This was eliminated in 4.2BSD; a user is now in all his or her groups at once, and the processes he or she executes have the permissions associated with all the groups instead of only one at a time.

In order to manipulate the new group mechanism, two new system calls have been provided. getgroups takes two arguments, a pointer to an array of integers and the number of elements in that array. The number of elements is passed as the first argument. It returns the number of groups the calling process is in; the group ids of these groups are placed in the array. −1 is returned if an error occurs, and errno will indicate the problem. setgroups also takes two arguments, the number of groups to place the calling process in, and a pointer to an array of integers containing the group ids of those groups. 0 is returned if all went well; otherwise −1 is returned and errno is set to the cause of the error. The number of groups may not exceed the constant NGROUPS, defined in *sys/param.h*.* Only the super-user may set new groups.

A library routine, initgroups, is also provided for use in programs such as *login*. This routine is called with two arguments; a login name and a base group id. It reads the group file searching for groups whose members include the given login name. It then calls setgroups with the group ids of these groups and the base group id. The base group id is normally the user's group id obtained from the password file, although this is not a requirement.

Reading the Password File

The password file contains almost all the information commonly maintained about each user of the system. Normally this file resides in */etc/passwd*. Each line in the file describes a separate user. The line is divided into several colon-separated fields; additionally the pw_gecos field (see below) is subdivided into several comma-separated fields.† The include file *pwd.h* describes the format of the password file to programs:

```
struct passwd {
    char    *pw_name;
    char    *pw_passwd;
    int     pw_uid;
    int     pw_gid;
    int     pw_quota;
    char    *pw_comment;
    char    *pw_gecos;
    char    *pw_dir;
```

---

*In the 4.2BSD setgroups documentation, this constant is incorrectly called NGRPS.
†For simplicity, this book will describe the Berkeley UNIX format of pw_gecos. The reader should be aware that this field's format often varies to support local needs.

```
        char    *pw_shell;
    };
```

The fields are:

pw_name   The user's login name.

pw_passwd The user's encrypted password. Passwords are encrypted using
           the crypt library routine, not described in this book.

pw_uid   The user's numeric user id.

pw_gid   The user's numeric group id. This is conventionally called the
           user's *login group*, and is the group he is made a member of
           when he logs in.

pw_quota   This field is unused.

pw_comment This field is unused.

pw_gecos   The user's full name and other personal data. This field con-
           sists of four comma-separated subfields. By convention the
           first field is the user's name; an ampersand ('&') character is
           used to stand for the login name. Thus, a user whose login
           name is "smith" and whose full name is John Nesmith could
           be represented as "John Ne&". The second field is the user's
           office telephone number. The third is his or her office room
           number, and the last is his or her home telephone number. Any
           or all of these fields may be left blank.

pw_dir   The user's home directory.

pw_shell   The name of the program to execute when the user logs in.
           This is conventionally called his or her *login shell*. If left
           blank, the program */bin/sh* is assumed.

Several routines are provided to read the password file; all of them return a
pointer to a structure of type passwd, or NULL on end-of-file or error ("entry
not found" is considered an error). The pointer returned points to static data that
is overwritten with each call; programs must copy the data into another structure
if it is to be saved. The getpwent routine returns the next entry in the password file, reading sequentially from the beginning. getpwuid takes a numeric
user id as an argument and returns the entry for that user id. getpwnam takes a
pointer to a string containing a login name as an argument, and returns the entry
for that login name.

The routines setpwent and endpwent are used to open and close the password file, respectively. These should be used to "reset" the getpwent routine.
4.3BSD provides a routine, setpwfile, which takes the name of an alternate
password file as an argument; it is useful when reading other files of the same

format. System V performs this function in a different way; the `fgetpwent` routine takes an open file pointer as an argument and reads a password entry from that file. Note that this does not permit the use of the `getpwuid` and `getpwnam` routines as the Berkeley UNIX method does.

The `getpw` routine is often used in older code to read the password file. This routine is made obsolete by `getpwuid`, but is still provided for backward compatibility. It takes two arguments, an integer user id and a pointer to a character array. On successful return, the character array will contain a copy of the password file line for that user id and the routine returns 0. If the user id is not found, the routine returns non-zero.

Reading the Group File

The group file, *letc/group*, also contains lines of colon-separated fields. These lines are described by the `group` structure, defined in the include file *grp.h*:

```
struct group {
    char    *gr_name;
    char    *gr_passwd;
    int     gr_gid;
    char    **gr_mem;
};
```

The fields are:

`gr_name` The name of the group.

`gr_passwd` The encrypted password for the group. This field is almost always left blank. If non-blank, then the `newgrp` command prompts for a password before permitting a user to change to this group. Because of the new group mechanism, this field is meaningless in Berkeley UNIX.

`gr_gid` The numeric group id of the group.

`gr_mem` Pointers to the login names of the members of the group. The list is null-terminated.

The routines to read the group file are patterned directly after those to read the password file. All the routines return a pointer to a structure of type `group` or NULL on error. The routines are called `getgrent`, `getgrgid`, and `getgrnam`. The routines `setgrent` and `endgrent` are also available, although `setgrfile` and `fgetgrent` do not exist.

Reading the utmp File

The file */etc/utmp* contains a record of all users currently logged in on the system.* This file is usually ordered by tty number; each record is a structure of type utmp. This structure is defined in the include file *utmp.h* :

```
struct utmp {
    char    ut_line[8];    /* tty name */
    char    ut_name[8];    /* user id  */
    long    ut_time;       /* time on  */
};
```

The fields are:

ut_line   The terminal name the user is logged in on. Concatenating this with "/dev/" produces a legitimate path name. It is not guaranteed to be null-terminated.

ut_name   The user's login name. It is not guaranteed to be null-terminated. If ut_name[0] is null, the terminal is not logged in.

ut_time   The time the terminal was logged in, in standard UNIX time format.†

The structure described above is a common subset among all versions of UNIX. In Berkeley UNIX another field, ut_host, contains the name of the remote host for users logged in through the network.

The conventional way to read */etc/utmp* is simply to open it and read in structures. On non-System V systems, this is done using either low-level I/O or the stdio routines. System V, because it has extended the purpose of utmp, has provided a set of library routines to read the file, although using them is not required. Briefly, getutent returns a pointer to a structure of type utmp, the next one in the file. getutline takes a pointer to a utmp structure as an argument, and returns a pointer to a structure whose ut_line field matches that of the argument structure. The setutent and endutent routines are also available, as are some routines not described here.

The file */usr/adm/wtmp* (on System V, this has been moved to */etc*) contains a record of all users who have ever logged in on the system. Reading from the beginning, an entry whose ut_name field is non-zero indicates a login. An entry whose ut_name field is null indicates the time that terminal was logged off. There are other entries with special login names indicating system reboots,

---

*System V has modified this file to store all sorts of other information. This will not be discussed here.
†See Chapter 7, *Telling Time and Timing Things*.

shutdowns, etc.; these are version-specific. For more information about them, see the manual page for *wtmp*(5).

Example 6-1 shows a program that reads */etc/utmp* , and for every user logged in prints out their login name, their full name, the terminal they are logged in on, and the time they logged in.

Example 6-1. who—show who's on the system

```c
#include <stdio.h>
#include <utmp.h>
#include <pwd.h>

#define UTMP    "/etc/utmp"
#define NAMELEN    8

main()
{
    FILE *fp;
    struct utmp u;
    struct passwd *p;
    char tmp[NAMELEN+1];
    struct passwd *getpwnam();

    if ((fp = fopen(UTMP, "r")) == NULL) {
        perror(UTMP);
        exit(1);
    }

    /*
     * For each entry...
     */
    while (fread((char *)&u, sizeof(u), 1, fp) != NULL) {
        /*
         * Skip non-logged in ports.
         */
        if (u.ut_name[0] == NULL)
            continue;

        /*
         * Make sure name is null-terminated.
         */
        strncpy(tmp, u.ut_name, NAMELEN);

        /*
         * Skip non-existent users (shouldn't
         * be any).
         */
        if ((p = getpwnam(tmp)) == NULL)
            continue;

        /*
```

```
                * Print the line.  ctime() converts the time
                * to ASCII format, it is described in Chapter
                * 7, Telling Time and Timing Things. We
                * ignore the format of the gecos field and
                * just print the first 30 characters; in real
                * life we would stop at a comma or some such.
                */
               printf("%-10.8s %-10.8s %-30.30s %s", u.ut_name,
               u.ut_line, p->pw_gecos, ctime(&u.ut_time));
        }

        fclose(fp);
        exit(0);
}
```

7

Telling Time and Timing Things

Telling Time
Sleeping and Alarm Clocks
Process Timing
Changing File Times

This chapter covers a miscellany of topics unrelated but for the fact that they have to do with time:

- How the UNIX system keeps track of time.
- How to put processes to sleep.
- How to determine how much CPU time a process uses.
- How to change file modification times.

Telling Time

The UNIX operating system keeps track of the current date and time by storing the number of seconds that have elapsed since midnight January 1, 1970 UTC (Coordinated Universal Time, also known as Greenwich Mean Time). This date is considered the informal "birthday" of the UNIX operating system. The time is stored in a signed long integer.*

---

*For those who care, assuming a 32-bit signed integer, UNIX time will break at 03:14:08 January 19,

Obtaining the Time

In all versions of UNIX, the time system call may be used to obtain the time of day. This call is peculiar in that if given the address of a long integer as an argument, it places the time in that integer and returns it. If, however a null pointer is passed, the time of day is just returned.

In 4.2BSD, time was made into a library routine. It was replaced by the gettimeofday system call, which returns time in terms of seconds and microseconds. gettimeofday takes two arguments; a pointer to a structure of type timeval, and a pointer to a structure of type timezone. These are defined in the include file *sys/time.h* :*

```
struct timeval {
    long    tv_sec;         /* seconds              */
    long    tv_usec;        /* and microseconds     */
};

struct timezone {
    int     tz_minuteswest; /* mins west of UTC */
    int     tz_dsttime;     /* dst correction   */
};
```

The field tv_sec is the equivalent of the long integer passed to time. In order to simplify the rest of this discussion, we will assume the use of time instead of gettimeofday.

Timezones

Depending on the version of the operating system being used, the timezone is obtainable in several different ways. In Berkeley UNIX, it is obtained via the gettimeofday system call. In System V, it is stored as an environment variable, TZ (see Chapter 14, *Miscellaneous Routines*). In Version 7 and pre-4.2BSD versions of UNIX, it is obtained with the ftime system call. Fortunately, however, programs rarely need the timezone information themselves. The library routines that convert the long integer into an ASCII date string all obtain the timezone information internally.

2038 UTC.

*The file *time.h* is constantly moving back and forth between *time.h* and *sys/time.h* depending on which release of the operating system is used. From now on, we will refer to it as *time.h*, since this is the more often used location.

Converting the Time to ASCII

Several routines are available to convert the long integer returned by time into an ASCII date string. With the UNIX operating system, an ASCII date string is a 26-character string as shown below ("•" represents a space character):

```
Day•Mon•dd•hh:mm:ss•yyyy\n\0
```

For example, "Mon Dec 19 10:40:37 1988".

The time of day may be broken into its component parts using the gmtime and localtime routines. Both routines take a pointer to the long integer as an argument, and return a pointer to a structure of type tm, defined in the include file *time.h*:

```
struct tm {
        int     tm_sec;         /* seconds 0-59          */
        int     tm_min;         /* minutes 0-59          */
        int     tm_hour;        /* hours 0-23            */
        int     tm_mday;        /* day of month 1-31     */
        int     tm_mon;         /* month 0-11            */
        int     tm_year;        /* year-1900             */
        int     tm_wday;        /* day of week Sun=0     */
        int     tm_yday;        /* day of year 0-365     */
        int     tm_isdst;       /* 1 if daylight savings */
};
```

gmtime returns Coordinated Universal Time; localtime returns the time in the local time zone. The pointer to the tm structure may then be passed to the asctime routine, which returns a pointer to the character array containing the ASCII date string. For convenience, the ctime routine may be used when only the date string is required; it takes a pointer to the long integer as an argument.

To obtain the abbreviation for the local (or any other) timezone, the timezone routine should be used. It takes two arguments: the number of minutes west of UTC, and a flag indicating daylight savings time (non-zero). It returns a pointer to a character array containing the timezone abbreviation (EST, GMT, etc.).

All the routines described in this section return pointers to static data which is overwritten on each call.

Time Differences

By using the asctime and gmtime routines, it is possible to convert the difference between two times to ASCII. For example, to see how long a user was logged in, his login time can be subtracted from his logout time. This difference can then be taken as Universal Time, and converted to as ASCII string. The hours, minutes, and seconds fields of this result will represent the difference between the two times (modulo 24 hours).

```
session = logouttime-logintime;
printf("%.8s", asctime(gmtime(&session))+11);
```

Sleeping and Alarm Clocks

Sleeping

Many times it is necessary for a program to "go to sleep" for a period of time. For example, if some condition must be checked every 20 minutes, the program performs its checks and then must wait for 20 minutes before checking things again. The simplest way to do this is to use the sleep system call; it takes a single argument, the number of seconds to sleep. When that many seconds have elapsed, the call returns.

The Alarm Clock

Another common need is to be advised when a given amount of time has elapsed, but to be able to continue executing. For example, if a program is waiting for something that "might" happen, it needs to know when it has waited long enough and should give up. To schedule an alarm, the alarm system call should be used. It takes a single argument, the number of seconds between "now" and the time the alarm should be delivered. A value of 0 disables a scheduled alarm; only one alarm may be pending at any one time. The alarm is delivered in the form of the SIGALRM signal.*

Interval Timers

In 4.2BSD, sleep and alarm were replaced with a more general mechanism called *interval timers* (sleep and alarm remain as compatibility library routines). Interval timers are maintained in structures of type itimerval, defined in the include file *sys/time.h*:

---

*See Chapter 8, *Processing Signals*.

```
struct itimerval {
    struct timeval it_interval;   /* timer interval */
    struct timeval it_value;      /* current value  */
};
```

The `it_interval` field specifies the number of seconds and microseconds before the timer should expire; if these values are zero the timer is disabled. `it_value` specifies the values the timer should be reset to when it expires; if these are zero the timer will not be reset.

The three timers are accessed using the constants discussed below, also defined in *sys/time.h* .

ITIMER_REAL   The timer decrements in real (actual clock) time. When it expires, a SIGALRM signal is delivered to the process.

ITIMER_VIRTUAL   The timer decrements in process virtual time. It runs only when the process is executing. When it expires, a SIGVTALRM signal is delivered to the process.

ITIMER_PROF   The timer decrements both in process virtual time and when the system is executing on behalf of the process. It is designed to be used by process-profiling programs. When it expires, a SIGPROF signal is delivered to the process. Because this timer is capable of interrupting system calls, the process using it should be prepared to restart these system calls.

The `getitimer` call takes two arguments: the first is one of the constants above, indicating which timer to use, and the second is a pointer to an `itimerval` structure. The current value of the timer is returned in the structure. If the call succeeds, 0 is returned; otherwise -1 is returned and `errno` will contain the reason for failure.

To set an interval timer, `setitimer` is used. It takes three arguments: one of the constants above indicating which timer to set, a pointer to an `itimerval` structure containing the new values to be set, and a pointer to another `itimerval` structure, in which the current setting of the timer will be returned. The third pointer may be null, in which case the old value is not returned. If the call succeeds, 0 is returned; −1 is returned and `errno` is set if an error occurs.

Using the real-time interval timer, it is possible to create a routine `nap`, which sleeps for sixtieths of a second. This is sometimes desirable when working with devices, etc. Before 4.2BSD, `nap` had to be implemented locally as a system call. For convenience, a listing of the interval timer implementation of `nap` is provided in Appendix E, *Interval Timer Version of nap()*.

Process Timing

To obtain information about the amount of processor time used by a process, the
`times` system call may be used. This call takes a single argument, a pointer to a
structure of type `tms`. This structure is defined in the include file *sys/times.h*; the
inclusion of *sys/types.h* is also necessary.

```
struct tms {
        time_t      tms_utime;      /* user time                */
        time_t      tms_stime;      /* system time              */
        time_t      tms_cutime;     /* user time, children      */
        time_t      tms_cstime;     /* system time, children */
};
```

`tms_utime` and `tms_stime` contain the number of seconds of user and system time used by the process itself. `tms_cutime` and `tms_cstime` contain
the number of seconds of user and system time used by the process's children. It
should be noted that a process inherits the time used by its children, so technically the amount of user time used by the parent process is equal to:

```
tms_utime - tms_cutime
```

User time is the time spent by the CPU executing in user mode. This is time spent
adding numbers, comparing, running user-level routines, etc. *System time* is the
time spent by the CPU executing in kernel mode. This is time spent by the operating system executing on behalf of the process. Simply put, system time is the
amount of time spent doing system calls, user time is all the other time spent executing.

In 4.0 and 4.1BSD, an additional system call, `vtimes`, was added to provide
more precise information about execution times. In 4.2BSD, `times` and
`vtimes` were replaced with the more general `getrusage` system call (the
other calls remain as library routines for compatibility). Since most of the information returned by `getrusage` is not related to process timing, discussion of
this call is deferred to Chapter 14, *Miscellaneous Routines*.

Example 7-1 shows the proper method to calculate the amount of CPU time
required by a given segment of code:

Example 7-1. cputime—measure cpu time used by a section of code

```
#include <sys/types.h>
#include <sys/times.h>

main()
{
```

```
struct tms before, after;

times(&before);

/* ... place code to be timed here ... */

times(&after);

printf("User time: %ld seconds\n", after.tms_utime -
    before.tms_utime);
printf("System time: %ld seconds\n", after.tms_stime -
    before.tms_stime);

exit(0);
}
```

Changing File Times

It is possible to change the access and modification times on a file (but not the i-node change time) to arbitrary values using the utime system call. This call takes two arguments: a pointer to the character string containing the name of the file to change, and a pointer to an array of two long integers containing the new values for the access and modification times, respectively. The i-node change time will be set to the current time.

In Berkeley UNIX, utime is now a library routine; it has been replaced by utimes. This call takes a pointer to an array of two timeval structures instead of two long integers.

8

Processing Signals

Overview of Signal Handling
The Signals
Sending Signals
Catching and Ignoring Signals
Using Signals for Timeouts
The New Berkeley UNIX Signal Mecha-
nism

Signals are "software interrupts" that are delivered to processes to inform them of abnormal events occurring in their environment. Some signals, such as "floating point exception," have direct counterparts in the computer hardware; other signals, such as "change in child process status," are purely software-oriented. Most of the standard UNIX signals cause a process to terminate when they are received. Depending on the signal, the memory image of the executing process may be placed on the disk in the file *core*. This is the familiar *core dump*; it is often useful when debugging a broken program.

Overview of Signal Handling

The operating system permits a process to do one of three things with signals. Each signal may be treated individually in one of the following ways:

- The signal may be *ignored*. This causes the operating system to refrain from delivering the signal to the process. Programs often ignore the "interrupt" and "quit" signals, which are the only process-terminating signals you may generate from the keyboard.

- The signal may be *caught*. This is also referred to as *trapping* a signal. Catching a signal involves specifying to the operating system a user-supplied procedure that should be called on delivery of the signal. Execution of the process transfers to this routine when the signal arrives, and when the routine returns it returns to the point at which it was called; this is described later in this chapter.

- The signal may be set to a *default*. That is, after informing the operating system that it wishes to catch or ignore a signal, a process may "change its mind" and restore the default action of the signal.

In 4.2BSD, two very important features of the mechanism were changed in order to provide a more versatile interface (and one that more closely emulates hardware interrupts). This change brought about severe criticism from many members of the UNIX community, mostly from those members whose programs broke under the new mechanism. 4.3BSD has attempted to pacify the objectors to some extent by making the features selectable.

Resetting Signals

In Version 7, System V, and pre-4.2BSD versions of UNIX, signals that are being caught are reset to their default actions before the user's routine is called. This means that your routine must issue another request to catch the signal if all such signals are to be caught. Conventionally, signal handlers issue a request to ignore the signal as their first statement, and then issue a new catch request immediately before returning. This behavior makes it very difficult to write "impenetrable" programs, since by sending signals rapid-fire at a process it is possible to eventually catch it between the point that the signal is reset to its default and the point that the process issues another request to ignore the signal.

In 4.2BSD, signals are not reset when they are caught. Rather, when the user routine is called, all further occurrences of that signal are blocked until the routine returns. At that time, the signal is reset to call the user's routine when another signal is delivered. This change can affect pre-4.2BSD programs that rely on the signal being reset to its default value after the call or those that preferred to handle each occurrence of the interrupt separately (even those that arrived while the process was already handling a previous interrupt).

Restarting System Calls

In the pre-4.2BSD versions of UNIX, a system call in progress when a signal is received will be aborted. In particular, this can happen during reads and writes to slow devices such as terminals (but not to fast devices such as disks). When the user's signal handling routine returns, the system call will return a –1 as though an error has occurred, and `errno` will be set to `EINTR`. This makes it easy to write code that "times out" when reading from terminals and so on by using the alarm mechanism alluded to earlier, but such behavior is not always desirable.

4.2BSD provides restartable system calls. If a process is interrupted during a system call, the system call will be restarted when the user's handling routine returns. This behavior is often desirable, but it caused several programs attempting to "time out" on various operations to break when 4.2BSD was first released.

4.3BSD permits you to select, on a signal-by-signal basis, whether or not interrupted system calls will be restarted.

The Signals

Version 7 provided 15 signals. Berkeley UNIX extended that set with 4.0 and 4.1BSD, until now in 4.3BSD there are 30 signals. System V has added four more signals to the original 15 for a total of 19. Various ports of UNIX by different vendors provide other signals related to their machines; in particular the real-time versions of UNIX will have other signals.

The list below names all signals available in the AT&T and Berkeley releases of the operating system. Signals marked with ♥ cause the process to dump core; those marked with ♦ are discarded (never delivered) unless the process is catching them. Signals marked with ♠ cause the process to stop when they are received. Signals marked with ♣ are available only on Berkeley UNIX systems, while signals marked with ★ are available only under System V.

SIGHUP	Hangup. This is sent to processes when their controlling terminal hangs up the phone line.
SIGINT	Interrupt. This is one of the keyboard-generated interrupts.
SIGQUIT ♥	Quit. This is another of the keyboard-generated interrupts.
SIGILL ♥	Illegal Instruction. Not reset when caught on non-4.2BSD systems.

SIGTRAP ♥	Trace trap. Not reset when caught on non-4.2BSD systems.
SIGIOT ♥	IOT (I/O) trap.
SIGEMT ♥	EMT (emulator) trap.
SIGFPE ♥	Floating point exception (divide by zero, overflow, underflow).
SIGKILL	Kill. This signal cannot be caught, blocked or ignored.
SIGBUS ♥	Bus error.
SIGSEGV ♥	Segmentation violation.
SIGSYS ♥	Bad argument to system call.
SIGPIPE	Write on a pipe with no one to read it.
SIGALRM	Alarm clock.
SIGTERM	Software termination signal.
SIGURG ♦♣	Urgent condition present on socket (4.2 and 4.3BSD).
SIGSTOP ♠♣	Stop. This signal cannot be caught, blocked or ignored.
SIGTSTP ♠♣	Stop signal generated from keyboard.
SIGCONT ♦♣	Continue after a stop. This signal cannot be blocked.
SIGCHLD ♦♣	Child process status has changed.
SIGTTIN ♠♣	Background read attempted from control terminal.
SIGTTOU ♠♣	Background write attempted to control terminal.
SIGIO ♦♣	I/O possible on a descriptor.
SIGXCPU ♣	CPU time limit exceeded.
SIGXFSZ ♣	File size limit exceeded.
SIGVTALRM ♣	Virtual timer alarm (4.2 and 4.3BSD).
SIGPROF ♣	Profiling timer alarm (4.2 and 4.3BSD).
SIGWINCH ♦♣	Window changed size (4.3BSD only).
SIGCLD ♦☆	Death of a child.
SIGPWR ♦☆	Power failure.
SIGUSR1	User-defined signal 1 (4.3BSD and System V).
SIGUSR2	User-defined signal 2 (4.3BSD and System V).

Because they are handled somewhat differently than other signals, discussion of `SIGSTOP`, `SIGTSTP`, `SIGTTIN`, `SIGTTOU`, and `SIGCONT` will be postponed until Chapter 10, *Job Control*. The rest of this chapter discusses signal handling with respect to `SIGHUP`, `SIGINT`, and `SIGALRM`.

Sending Signals

The system call used for delivering signals to processes is called `kill`, and takes two arguments. The first argument, *pid*, is an integer indicating the *process id* of the process which is to receive the signal. The second argument, *sig*, is a signal number, as defined in the previous section. The real or effective user id of the sending process must match that of the receiving process unless the effective user id of the sender is super-user.

If *pid* is 0, the signal is sent to all other processes in the sender's process group.*

If *pid* is –1, and the effective user id of the sending process is super-user, the signal is broadcast universally to all processes in the system except system processes and the process sending the signal. If *pid* is –1, and the effective user id of the sending process is not super-user, the signal is broadcast universally to all processes with the same user id as the sender except the process sending the signal.

If *pid* is negative, but not equal to –1, the signal is sent to all processes whose process group id is equal to the absolute value of *pid*.

If *sig* is 0, no signal is sent, but error checking is performed.† Programs that monitor the system to make sure that all the appropriate service programs are still operating can make use of this feature to check that a program (with a known process id) is still running.

Processes may send signals to themselves.

Catching and Ignoring Signals

The system call used to process signals is called `signal`; it takes two arguments. The first argument is the name of the signal as shown in the previous section; these constants are defined in the include file *signal.h*. The second argument may be either SIG_DFL to indicate that the signal should behave in the default manner, SIG_IGN to indicate that the signal should be ignored, or a pointer to a routine to be called when the signal is received. The previous "value" of the signal is returned if the call succeeds; –1 is returned on error and `errno` will contain a more specific cause for failure.

---

*Process groups are described in Chapter 10, *Job Control*.
†This feature is not available in all versions of the UNIX operating system, although it exists in 4.2BSD, 4.3BSD, and System V.

The bulk of the discussion in this chapter is presented using `signal`. This routine is truly a system call on all versions of UNIX except 4.2 and 4.3BSD, where it is provided as a compatibility library routine. The new 4.2BSD signal mechanism is much more powerful than the `signal` interface. However, it is also more complex. For this reason, discussion of the system calls `sigvec`, `sigblock`, `sigpause`, `sigsetmask`, and `sigstack` is deferred until later in the chapter, where the discussion can build on the information presented about `signal`.

Ignoring Signals

To ignore a signal, the call:

```
signal(signame, SIG_IGN)
```

should be used. This causes all occurrences of the signal to be ignored until the process resets the action to something else. Example 8-1 shows a small program that ignores the interrupt signal. This program can be executed, and the interrupt key may be pressed, but it will have no effect (use the quit key to get out of the program).

Example 8-1. ignoreint—a program which ignores the interrupt signal

```
#include <signal.h>

main()
{
    signal(SIGINT, SIG_IGN);

    /*
     * pause() just suspends the process until a
     * signal is received.
     */
    pause();
}
```

The standard command interpreters (the Bourne and C shells) issue calls to ignore the keyboard-generated signals when a process is started in the background. If they didn't, then striking the interrupt key would terminate background processes as well as the intended process. This is because signals generated from the keyboard are normally sent to all processes started from the terminal (the *controlling terminal* of the process).*

---

*Actually, newer versions of the UNIX operating system send signals only to the processes in the controlling terminal's process group; this will be described in more detail in Chapter 10, *Job Control*.

Catching Signals

A signal can be caught and handled by a user routine by supplying a pointer to that routine in the `signal` call.* The first time the signal is received, this routine will be called to process that signal. When the routine (commonly called a *signal handler*) is called, it will be passed a single integer argument indicating which signal was received. This integer can be compared against the constants in *signal.h*, enabling the programmer to write general-purpose signal handlers.

Example 8-2 shows a small program that catches the interrupt signal and prints the string "OUCH" when it is received. On non-Berkeley systems, pressing interrupt a second time will break out of the program since the signal was not reset.

Example 8-2. ouch1—prints "ouch" when an interrupt is received

```
#include <signal.h>

main()
{
    /*
     * Declare handler routine so we can use its name.
     */
    extern int handler();

    /*
     * Send signal to handler routine.
     */
    signal(SIGINT, handler);

    /*
     * Loop here.
     */
    for (;;)
        pause();
}

/*
 * handler--handle the signal.
 */
handler()
{
    /*
     * Users of 4.2 and 4.3BSD systems should un-comment
     * this line, which will make this program
     * behave as if it were on a non-Berkeley system.
```

---

*A pointer to a routine is simply the routine's name; see Chapter 5 of *The C Programming Language*, by Brian Kernighan and Dennis Ritchie.

```
     */
    /* signal(SIGINT, SIG_DFL); */

    printf("OUCH\n");
}
```

Example 8-3 shows the same program with one line of code added to reset the signal. This program will print "OUCH" every time the interrupt key is pressed. On Berkeley systems, the two programs will behave identically; the example shows how to make the program "pretend" it is on a non-Berkeley system.

Example 8-3. ouch2—prints "ouch" when interrupt is received

```
#include <signal.h>

main()
{
    /*
     * Declare handler routine so we can use its
     * name.
     */
    extern int handler();

    /*
     * Send signal to handler routine.
     */
    signal(SIGINT, handler);

    /*
     * Loop here.
     */
    for (;;)
        pause();
}

/*
 * handler—handle the signal.
 */
handler()
{
    /*
     * Users of 4.2 and 4.3BSD systems should un-comment
     * this line, which will make this program
     * behave as if it were on a non-Berkeley system.
     */
    /* signal(SIGINT, SIG_DFL); */

    printf("OUCH\n");

    /*
     * Reset the signal to come here again.
     */
```

```
        signal(SIGINT, handler);
}
```

Although it works well enough when testing, Example 8-3 has two serious problems that are not obvious but are important to handle. First, recall that on non-Berkeley systems a signal is reset to its default action *before* the user's routine to handle that signal is invoked. In the case of Example 8-3, this means that if you were to press the interrupt key while the program was in handler, the program would terminate. In this case, because the handler routine is so short, chances of this happening are small. However, if the handler routine were to perform some time-consuming computations, the chances of it being interrupted are very real. The solution, of course, is to add a call to signal on entry to the handler routine to ignore each signal the handler processes. A simpler method, and one that permits the handler routine to be used for any given signal, is to take advantage of the fact that the routine is passed the signal that interrupted the process as an argument. The improved routine is shown in Example 8-4.

The second problem with Example 8-3 involves the code that causes the interrupt signal to be caught in the first place. Recall that signals generated from the keyboard are sent to all processes started from the terminal. The shell takes special care to ignore these signals in processes started in the background (with the "&"). Because the first action of the program in Example 8-3 undoes this behavior, the program will print "OUCH" even if it is started in the background. (Try it!)* The solution is to test the current "value" of a signal before setting it, and change it only if the value is not SIG_IGN. This test is performed by setting the signal to be ignored, and saving the return value from the call. The improved program is shown in Example 8-4.

Example 8-4. ouch3—prints "ouch" when interrupt is received

```
#include <signal.h>

main()
{
    /*
     * Declare handler routine so we can use its
     * name.
     */
    extern int handler();
    /*
     * Send signal to handler routine.  Only do so
     * if the signal is not already being ignored.
     */
    if (signal(SIGINT, SIG_IGN) != SIG_IGN)
```

---

*Because the C-shell (**csh**) uses process groups, as discussed in Chapter 10, *Job Control*, this problem is only present in processes started from the Bourne shell (**sh**).

```
        signal(SIGINT, handler);

    /*
     * Loop here.
     */
    for (;;)
        pause();
}

/*
 * handler--handle the signal.  sig is the signal
 *           number which interrupted us.
 */
handler(sig)
int sig;
{
    /*
     * Users of 4.2 and 4.3BSD systems should un-comment
     * this line, which will make this program
     * behave as if it were on a non-Berkeley
     * system (we reset the signal by hand).
     */
    /* signal(sig, SIG_DFL); */

    /*
     * Ignore the signal for the duration of this
     * routine.
     */
    signal(sig, SIG_IGN);

    printf("OUCH\n");

    /*
     * Reset the signal to come here again.
     */
    signal(SIGINT, handler);
}
```

Using Signals for Timeouts

By using the alarm system call, a program can generate timeouts while performing various functions. For example, a program that wishes to read from a terminal, but give up after 30 seconds and take a default action, would issue an alarm
request for 30 seconds immediately before starting the read. When 30 seconds elapsed, a SIGALRM signal would be sent to the process.

On non-Berkeley systems, if the alarm signal is sent while the process is trying to read from the terminal, after the user's signal handling routine returns the read will return -1 and errno will be set to EINTR. The program can then take its default action. In 4.2BSD and 4.3BSD, because system calls are restarted, this timeout mechanism fails. When the user's signal handler returns, the read will be restarted, and the program will be back where it was before the alarm was generated. In 4.3BSD it is possible to make signals interrupt system calls instead of restart them; this is described later in this chapter. For the general case, however, the next section describes the proper way to write timeout routines that are portable between different versions of the UNIX operating system, regardless of whether or not interrupted system calls are restarted.

The setjmp and longjmp Routines

The setjmp and longjmp routines provide a program with a method for making a "non-local goto" to other parts of the program. This is done by saving the contents of the stack, and later "rewinding" the stack and restoring its contents from the saved information. setjmp takes a single argument, *env*, of type jmp_buf. This type is defined in the include file *setjmp.h*. longjmp takes two arguments, *env* and an integer *val*.

When setjmp is called, it saves the current stack environment in *env* and returns the value 0. longjmp restores the stack environment last saved in *env*. It then returns in such a way that execution continues as if setjmp had just returned the value *val* to the function which invoked setjmp. Needless to say, the function that called setjmp cannot have returned before the call to longjmp is made, or great havoc will result.

An example should make things clearer. Example 8-5 shows a program that waits 15 seconds for you to type something. If nothing is typed, the program will assume a default response. The program works by calling setjmp and then scheduling an alarm. When the setjmp returns the first time, the code inside the if statement will be executed. After the alarm is delivered, the signal handler issues a call to longjmp and "returns" the value 1 to setjmp. This second return from setjmp will cause the code inside the else statement to be executed.

Example 8-5. timeout—program to demonstrate a timeout routine

```
#include <signal.h>
#include <setjmp.h>

/*
 * The environment for setjmp.
 */
```

```
jmp_buf env;

main()
{
    int i;
    char buf[160];
    extern int timeout();

    /*
     * Inform the system we want to catch the
     * alarm signal.
     */
    signal(SIGALRM, timeout);

    /*
     * The code inside the if gets executed the first
     * time through setjmp, the code inside the else
     * the second time.
     */
    if (setjmp(env) == 0) {
        /*
         * Issue a request for an alarm to be
         * delivered in 15 seconds.
         */
        alarm(15);

        /*
         * Prompt for input.
         */
        printf("Type a word; if you don't in 15 ");
        printf("seconds I'll use \"WORD\": ");
        (void) fgets(buf, sizeof(buf), stdin);
        /*
         * Turn off the alarm.
         */
        alarm(0);
    }
    else {
        /*
         * Assume the default.
         */
        strcpy(buf, "WORD");
    }

    printf("\nThe word is: %s\n", buf);
    exit(0);
}

/*
 * timeout-catch the signal.
 */
timeout(sig)
```

```
int sig;
{
    /*
     * Ignore the signal for the duration of this
     * routine.
     */
    signal(sig, SIG_IGN);

    /*
     * We would perform any timeout-related
     * functions here; in this case there
     * are none.
     */

    /*
     * Restore the action of the alarm signal.
     */
    signal(SIGALRM, timeout);

    /*
     * Return to the main routine at setjmp,
     * and make setjmp return 1.
     */
    longjmp(env, 1);
}
```

The New Berkeley UNIX Signal Mechanism

The new signal mechanism provided with 4.2BSD is manipulated using the `sigvec`, `sigblock`, `sigpause`, `sigsetmask`, and `sigstack` system calls. `signal` is implemented as a routine in the compatibility library. This section describes briefly the methods for using the new signal mechanism. For a more detailed description, see Section 2 of the *UNIX Programmer's Manual*.

The replacement routine for `signal` is `sigvec`. This call takes three arguments: the signal to be manipulated, a pointer to a structure of type `sigvec` containing the new information to be set for the signal, and another pointer to a structure of the same type, in which the current information about the signal will be returned. Either pointer may be null, indicating that the structure should not be used. The `sigvec` structure is defined in the include file *signal.h*. In 4.2BSD, the structure is defined as:

```
struct sigvec {
    int     (*sv_handler)();
    int     sv_mask;
    int     sv_onstack;
};
```

sv_handler is a pointer to the user's signal handling routine; it is the same as the second argument to signal. sv_mask is a bit mask of signals to be blocked for the duration of the signal handler (see below). If sv_onstack is 1, the system will deliver the signal to the process on a *signal stack* (see below).

In 4.3BSD, sv_onstack is now called sv_flags. The only two flags that may be used are SV_ONSTACK, which indicates the signal should be delivered on the signal stack, and SV_INTERRUPT, which indicates that this signal should interrupt system calls. The latter is used to make the new signal mechanism behave as in other versions of UNIX.

Handler Calling Conventions

Under the new signal mechanism, a user-defined signal handler is called with three arguments: an integer indicating the signal received, an integer indicating a code mapping the signal to a hardware trap, and a pointer to a structure of type sigcontext, described in *signal.h* . This structure describes the program context to be restored when the handler terminates; it contains the previous (before the handler was called) values of the stack pointer, program counter, etc. The context is for use by handlers that restore the context themselves as opposed to letting the system do it (an extremely unusual thing to do). The constants with which the second argument may be compared are somewhat machine dependent; they are described in *sigvec* (2) and defined in *signal.h* .

The Signal Mask

The process *signal mask* defines the set of signals currently blocked from delivery. If the ith bit in the mask is a 1, then signal number i is blocked from delivery. The ith bit is set by ORing in a 1 shifted left $i-1$ places:

```
1L << (i-1)
```

4.3BSD defines a macro, sigmask, to do this computation.

A signal that is blocked from delivery will be held by the system pending delivery to the process if the mask ever changes to allow delivery of the signal. Note that blocking a signal from delivery is *not* the same thing as ignoring the signal with SIG_IGN; an ignored signal will be discarded rather than held for possible delivery in the future.

To define a new signal mask, the sigsetmask system call is used. This call takes a single argument, the new mask to be installed. The old mask is returned. The sigblock system call adds the mask given as its argument to the current signal mask by ORing the two masks together. The old mask is returned.

When a signal is delivered to a process, a new signal mask is installed for the duration of the signal handling routine. This mask is formed by taking the current signal mask, adding the signal to be delivered, and ORing in the signal mask stored in sv_mask for this signal.

The sigpause system call is similar to pause, which was demonstrated in Example 8-1. It takes a single argument, a signal mask. When called, the new signal mask is installed and the process is suspended until a signal (one that is not blocked by the new mask) is received. The old signal mask is then restored and execution is continued.

sigpause is normally used when a process runs in an infinite loop looking for work. The signal that indicates there is work to do is blocked using sigblock while the process does its work, and when the work is finished, the process pauses awaiting more work using sigpause with the mask returned by sigblock. Example 8-6 shows a small program segment that demonstrates this.

Example 8-6. sigblock—demonstrate use of the sigblock *routine*

```
#include <signal.h>

main()
{
    long mask;

    /*
     * Block SIGIO, which will indicate more
     * work to be done.
     */
    mask = sigmask(SIGIO);

    for (;;) {
        /*
         * Go do work.
         */
        dowork();

        /*
         * Pause until we receive a signal.
         * SIGIO is not blocked in mask.
         */
        sigpause(mask);
    }
}
```

The Signal Stack

It is possible for a program to specify an alternate stack on which signals should be processed. This may be necessary if receipt of the signal can occur when the process stack is invalid. For example, if a process runs out of stack space, it must be terminated: since there is no stack space available, the stack cannot be extended to catch the signal. Using the alternate signal stack, the process can take the signal on this stack, issue the appropriate requests to increase the stack size limit, and then return to normal operation on the regular stack.

The signal stack is defined using the `sigstack` call which takes two arguments, both pointers to structures of type `sigstack`. The first structure indicates the new stack to be defined, the second is used to return information about the current stack. The `sigstack` structure is defined in *signal.h* as:

```
struct sigstack {
    char    *ss_sp;
    int     ss_onstack;
};
```

`ss_sp` is the stack pointer on the signal stack; when defining a new stack it should point to the beginning of the memory to be used for the stack. `ss_onstack` is non-zero if the process is currently executing on this stack, zero otherwise. The memory to be used for the signal stack *must* exist in the process' data space; i.e., it must be declared using the `brk` system call (or equivalently, the `alloc` family of library routines).

The process indicates to the system on a per signal basis whether that signal should be taken on the signal stack or the normal process stack. This is done using the `sigvec` system call as described previously. When the signal is delivered, the process will be executing on the signal stack for the duration of the signal handler. If the handler simply returns, it is best to allow the system to restore the process context from before the signal. If the handler performs a `longjmp` or other abnormal method of return, it should restore the context itself; this may only be done in a machine-dependent manner using assembly language and other nastiness.

Example 8-7 shows a program that limits its stack size to 50 kilobytes, and then calls a routine recursively until it runs out of stack space. When it runs out, the process will receive an illegal instruction signal. The process takes this signal on the signal stack, increases its stack size limit, and then returns; this permits the routine to continue recursing. The `setrlimit` system call is described in Chapter 14, *Miscellaneous Routines*.

Example 8-7. sigstack—demonstrate use of the signal stack

```
#include <sys/types.h>
#include <sys/time.h>
#include <sys/resource.h>
#include <signal.h>
#include <stdio.h>

char *stack;       /* pointer to signal stack base */
int tooksig = 0;   /* 1 after we take the signal   */

main()
{
    extern char * malloc ();
    extern int x();
    struct sigvec sv;
    struct sigstack ss;
    struct rlimit rlimit;

    /*
     * Set stack size limit to 50 kbytes.
     */
    getrlimit(RLIMIT_STACK, &rlimit);
    rlimit.rlim_cur = 50 * 1024;
    if (setrlimit(RLIMIT_STACK, &rlimit) < 0) {
        perror("setrlimit");
        exit(1);
    }

    /*
     * Take illegal instruction and process it with x,
     * on the interrupt stack.  For 4.2BSD, change
     * sv_flags to sv_onstack and SV_ONSTACK to 1.
     */
    sv.sv_mask = 0;
    sv.sv_handler = x;
    sv.sv_flags = SV_ONSTACK;
    sigvec(SIGILL, &sv, (struct sigvec *) 0);

    /*
     * Allocate memory for the signal stack.  The
     * kernel assumes the addresses grow in the same
     * direction as on the process stack (toward
     * lower addresses, on a VAX).
     */
    if ((stack = malloc(10240)) == NULL) {
        fprintf(stderr, "Out of memory.\n");
        exit(1);
    }

    /*
     * Issue the call to tell the system about the
     * signal stack.  We pass the end of the signal
```

```
      * stack, not the beginning, since the stack
      * grows toward lower addresses.
      */
     ss.ss_onstack = 0;
     ss.ss_sp = (caddr_t) stack + 10240;

     if (sigstack(&ss, (struct sigstack *) 0) < 0) {
         perror("sigstack");
         exit(1);
     }

     /*
      * Start using up stack space.
      */
     y();
}

y()
{
     /*
      * Take up 5k of stack space.
      */
     char buf[5120];

     printf("%s\n", tooksig ? "Now on extended stack." :
         "On 50k stack.");

     /*
      * Recurse.
      */
     y();
}

/*
 * Handle the signal.
 */
void x(sig, code, scp)
int sig, code;
struct sigcontext *scp;
{
     struct rlimit rlimit;

     /*
      * Increase the stack limit to the maximum.
      */
     getrlimit(RLIMIT_STACK, &rlimit);
     rlimit.rlim_cur = rlimit.rlim_max;

     if (setrlimit(RLIMIT_STACK, &rlimit) < 0) {
         perror("setrlimit");
         exit(1);
     }
```

```
        tooksig = 1;
        return;
}
```

Signals play an important role in UNIX programming, and it is important to understand them. This chapter has discussed several of the techniques and pitfalls associated with signal processing; Chapter 10, *Job Control*, discusses several more signals associated with Berkeley UNIX job control.

9

Executing Programs

The system Library Routine
Executing Programs Directly
Redirecting Input and Output
Setting Up Pipelines

One of the most powerful tools provided for the UNIX programmer is the ability to have one program execute another. For example, the command interpreter (shell) is a simple program like any other, which executes programs for the user. It is possible for anyone to write his or her own shell if he or she doesn't like the ones provided, and several people have. This chapter describes the methods used to execute programs from within other programs.

The system Library Routine

The simplest way to execute a program is by using the system library routine. This routine takes a single argument, a character string containing the command to be executed. This command string is passed directly to the UNIX Bourne shell, *sh*, where it is executed. Because it is being passed to the shell, the command string used with system may contain input and output redirection commands, as well as pipe constructs. The shell reads these commands and builds the appropriate connections between all the processes.

There are three major problems with system. First, it is not terribly versatile. Commands may be executed, but the process executing them has no control over the subprocess. Second, a lot of overhead is required. Before executing the desired command, system executes a Bourne shell process. Because the shell will immediately be executing something else, this is a waste of processor time. Third, system is a security hole. In order to prevent random system cracking, the security problems presented by system will not be described here. Suffice it to say that a set-user-id (particularly to the super-user) program should *never* use system to execute its sub-processes.

Executing Programs Directly

The alternative to using system is to create new processes and execute programs directly. There are three distinct steps to executing programs: creating new processes, making them execute other programs, and waiting for them to terminate.

In order to execute a program, it is first necessary to create a new process for that program to run in. A running program creates a new process by making a copy of itself. This copy is then immediately overlaid with the new program to be executed.

Creating Processes

The system call to create a new process is called fork. When executed, fork will make a copy of the current process that will have its own data space (i.e., if one process modifies a variable, it does not affect the variable in the other process), and the two processes will execute side by side. The process executing the call is called the *parent process*; the new process is called the *child process*. If the call fails, −1 is returned and the reason for failure is placed in errno.

fork is interesting in that it returns different values to the parent process and to the child process (this is how they tell themselves apart). fork will return to the parent process the process id of the child process. fork returns 0 to the child process. With the exception of this difference of return values, the two processes are now entirely identical.

Executing Programs

The system call used to execute programs is generically called exec. It exists in several forms described below, but all forms of the call share certain properties.

When an exec succeeds, the calling process is *overlaid* with the new program. That is, the memory being used by the caller is freed and the new program is loaded in its place. This means that once an exec succeeds, there can be no return to the calling process; it is gone forever. If the call fails, –1 is returned and errno will indicate the reason for failure.

Certain properties of the calling process are retained across an exec. First, all open files remain open and are referred to by the same file descriptor values, unless a file descriptor has its "close-on-exec" flag set. (This flag, which is set using the fcntl system call (see Chapter 5, *Device I/O Control*), indicates that the file descriptor it is associated with should be closed in the child process. This is useful when the parent process will be using files which the child should not have access to.)

Second, any signals being ignored by the calling process will remain ignored in the new program. Signals that were being trapped, however, will be restored to their default values (since the handler routines no longer exist). Finally, the real and effective user and group ids of the calling process are given to the new program, unless the new program has the set-user-id or set-group-id bits set, in which case its effective ids will be modified.

When a C program is executed, it is called as shown:

```
main(argc, argv, environ)
int argc;
char *argv[], *environ[];
```

where argc is the number of arguments including the program name, argv points to a null-terminated array of pointers to the arguments (the first element, *argv, is the name of the program), and environ points to a null-terminated array of environment variables and their values. Each of these array elements has the form NAME=*value*. The strings in argv and environ are all null-terminated; the arrays themselves contain null pointers to indicate the end of the list.

The primary form of the exec call is execve. The call takes three arguments: the first is a character string containing the path name of the program to be executed. The second argument is a pointer to the argument list, and the third is a pointer to the environment. This form of the call is used by the shell to provide environment variables to the programs it executes.

There are several other forms of exec described below. In all but the execle form of the call, the new program inherits its environment from the calling process.

execv   In this form of the call, the first argument is a character string indicating the path to the program to be executed. The second is a null-terminated array of pointers to the argument list; the first argument is conventionally the program name.

execl   In this form of the call, the first argument is again a character string naming the path to the program to be executed. Following this is a variable number of arguments, each of which will be given as an argument to the program. The second argument (first argument to the program) is conventionally the program name. The list of arguments should be null-terminated.

execvp Like execv, except that the first argument is searched for in the program's search path, and the first existing executable file by that name is executed.

execlp Like execl, except that the first argument is searched for in the program's search path, and the first existing executable file by that name is executed.

execle In this form of the call, the new environment is passed as a null-terminated array of pointers following the null argument terminating the argument list.

Waiting for Processes to Terminate

After spawning a new process, the parent process is free to go about its business. The two processes will be executing at the same time; neither will wait on the other. This is the way the shell starts up a process in the background; it simply spawns a new process which executes the new program, and the parent prints another prompt to you.

Unfortunately, the above is not always desirable. Often the parent cannot continue until the program the child executes has completed its work. For this reason, the wait system call is provided. wait takes a single argument, the address of an integer. This integer will contain the exit status of a child process when the call returns. When wait is executed, the process is delayed until a signal is received or one of its children exits. If a child has exited since the last wait, then return is immediate, returning the process id and exit status of one of the exited children.

Example 9-1 shows a program that reads commands from the terminal and executes them one at a time, waiting for the command to terminate before prompting for a new command. It should be noted that the code inside the if in execute is executed only by the child process. The calls to perror and exit will only be executed if the exec fails, since there is no return from a successful call to exec. The call to exit is important; if it wasn't there, then every time a program could not be executed another child process would remain. Execution would leave the if, and the child would begin executing the parent's code. The return value from wait is checked to insure that the exiting child process which terminated the wait is indeed the direct child of the parent. This is done because all processes, whether started by the parent or one of its children, can be waited on by the parent. If the child were to execute a program which terminated before the child itself, this would be the first process id returned by the call to wait.

Example 9-1. ezshell—a simple shell program

```
#include <stdio.h>

main()
{
    char buf[1024];
    char *args[64];

    for (;;) {
        /*
         * Prompt for and read a command.
         */
        printf("Command: ");

        if (fgets (buf, sizeof(buf), stdin) == NULL) {
            printf("\n");
            exit(0);
        }

        /*
         * Split the string into arguments.
         */
        parse(buf, args);

        /*
         * Execute the command.
         */
        execute(args);
    }
}

/*
 * parse--split the command in buf into
 *          individual arguments.
 */
```

```
parse(buf, args)
char *buf;
char **args;
{
    while (*buf != '\0') {
        /*
         * Strip whitespace.  Use nulls, so
         * that the previous argument is terminated
         * automatically.
         */
        while ((*buf == ' ') || (*buf == '\t') || (*buf == '\n'))
            *buf++ = '\0';

        /*
         * Save the argument.
         */
        *args++ = buf;

        /*
         * Skip over the argument.
         */
        while ((*buf != '\0') && (*buf != ' ')
            && (*buf != '\t') && (*buf != '\n')) buf++;
    }

    *args = '\0';
}

/*
 * execute--spawn a child process and execute
 *             the program.
 */
execute(args)
char **args;
{
    int pid, status;

    /*
     * Get a child process.
     */
    if ((pid = fork()) < 0) {
        perror("fork");
        exit(1);
    }

    /*
     * The child executes the code inside the if.
     */
    if (pid == 0) {
        execvp(*args, args);
        perror(*args);
        exit(1);
    }
```

```
/*
 * The parent executes the wait.
 */
while (wait(&status) != pid)
    /* empty */ ;
}
```

Redirecting Input and Output

Example 9-1 is useful, perhaps even as a very primitive shell. It reads a command from you, and then executes it. Unfortunately, there is no way to make the command read from a file, nor write to one as the real shell does. Fortunately, this is relatively easy to do.

Chapter 3, *Low-Level I/O*, described the dup system call, which could be used to obtain a new file descriptor referring to the same file as its argument. Further, as mentioned above, files stay open across calls to exec and child processes are identical in every way to their parents. This implies that to make a process read and write files instead of the terminal, it is only necessary to open the files and issue the appropriate calls to dup in the child process.

Example 9-2 shows a modified version of the execute routine from Example 9-1. This routine takes four arguments: the arguments to the program and file descriptors referring to the files which should be used as the new program's standard input, standard output, and standard error output. If no file is to be used, the caller of execute can simply pass down 0, 1, or 2 respectively. The program must check, however that it does not inadvertently close one of these descriptors, since the call to dup would then fail (in other words, it is not possible to make dup return its argument).

Example 9-2. execute— spawn a process and execute a program

```
execute(args, sin, sout, serr)
char **args;
int sin, sout, serr;
{
    int pid, status;

    /*
     * Get a child process.
     */
    if ((pid = fork()) < 0) {
        perror("fork");
        exit(1);
    }
```

```
/*
 * The child executes the code inside the if.
 */
if (pid == 0) {
    /*
     * For each of standard input, output,
     * and error output, set the child's
     * to the passed-down file descriptor.
     * Note that we can't just close 0, 1,
     * and 2 since we might need them.
     */
    if (sin != 0) {
        close(0);
        dup(sin);      /* will give us fd #0 */
    }

    if (sout != 1) {
        close(1);
        dup(sout);     /* will give us fd #1 */
    }

    if (serr != 2) {
        close(2);
        dup(serr);     /* will give us fd #2 */
    }

    execvp(*args, args);
    perror(*args);
    exit(1);
}

/*
 * The parent executes the wait.
 */
while (wait(&status) != pid)
    /* empty loop */;
}
```

There is a minor problem with this function: if the program redirects the standard error output to a file, and then the child cannot execute the new program, the `perror` call will write its error message on the file rather than the terminal. There are several ways to solve this problem; its solution is left as an exercise to you.

Setting Up Pipelines

One of the most powerful features of the UNIX operating system is the ability to constuct a pipeline of commands. This pipeline is set up such that the output of the first command is sent to the input of the second, the output of the second command is sent to the input of the third, and so forth. This eliminates the need to run each command separately, saving the intermediate results in temporary files.

The popen Library Routine

One way to create a pipe is to use popen. This routine takes two arguments: a character string containing the command to be executed, and a mode similar to that used with fopen. It calls the shell to execute the command just as system does, and then returns a file pointer which may be used to communicate with the process. When the program is done communicating with the process, it should close the pipe using pclose.

The popen routine has the same disadvantages that system does. For this reason, most programmers prefer to do their own "plumbing" in programs which will be used often.

Creating Pipes Directly

The system call to create a pipe is called pipe. It takes a single argument, an array of two integers. If the call succeeds, the array will contain two file descriptors to be used as the pipe; otherwise −1 is returned and errno indicates the reason for failure. After creating the pipe, a program should spawn a child process. The parent reads data from the child on the first descriptor, and writes data to the child on the second descriptor. Similarly, the child reads data from the parent on the first descriptor, and writes data to the parent on the second descriptor. It is common for the child to have its standard input and standard output connected to the first and second descriptors, respectively.

Example 9-3 shows a small program that opens a pipe to the electronic mail program and sends a message to the person executing it. The fdopen function takes a low-level file descriptor and a mode as arguments, and returns a stdio file pointer which refers to the same file. This enables programs to use low-level I/O routines for a time and then convert to high-level routines. Note that there is no real need for the parent to wait on the child process to terminate. In fact, deleting the wait has the advantage of making the child run in the background so that the user doesn't have to wait for it to finish. You are invited to modify this program to execute other programs and read from the pipe instead of writing, or perhaps both.

Example 9-3. mailer—open a pipe to the mail command and send mail

```
#include <stdio.h>

main()
{
    FILE *fp;
    int pid, pipefds[2];
    char *username, *getlogin();

    /*
     * Get the user's name.
     */
    if ((username = getlogin()) == NULL) {
        fprintf(stderr, "Who are you?\n");
        exit(1);
    }

    /*
     * Create the pipe.  This has to be done
     * BEFORE the fork.
     */
    if (pipe(pipefds) < 0) {
        perror("pipe");
        exit(1);
    }

    if ((pid = fork()) < 0) {
        perror("fork");
        exit(1);
    }

    /*
     * The child process executes the stuff inside
     * the if.
     */
    if (pid == 0) {
        /*
         * Make the read side of the pipe our
         * standard input.
         */
        close(0);
        dup(pipefds[0]);
        close(pipefds[0]);

        /*
         * Close the write side of the pipe;
         * we'll let our output go to the screen.
         */
```

```
        close(pipefds[1]);
        /*
         * Execute the command "mail username".
         */
        execl("/bin/mail", "mail", username, (char *) 0);
        perror("exec");
        exit(1);
    }

    /*
     * The parent executes this code.
     */

    /*
     * Close the read side of the pipe; we
     * don't need it (and the child is not
     * writing on the pipe anyway).
     */
    close(pipefds[0]);

    /*
     * Convert the write side of the pipe to stdio.
     */
    fp = fdopen(pipefds[1], "w");

    /*
     * Send a message, close the pipe.
     */
    fprintf(fp, "Hello from your program.\n");
    fclose(fp);

    /*
     * Wait for the process to terminate.
     */
    while (wait((int *) 0) != pid)
        ;

    exit(0);
}
```

10

Job Control

Preliminary Concepts
Job Control in the Shell
Job Control Outside the Shell
Important Points

The job control mechanism provided in Berkeley versions of the UNIX system enables a user to control many processes at once. Coupled with the commands provided by the C shell (*csh*) and the new tty driver, the job control mechanism enables you to:

- Suspend an executing job.
- Place that job in the background.
- Continue the job's execution.
- Return the job to the foreground.
- Cause a background job to be stopped when it attempts output to the terminal.
- Cause a background job to stop when it tries to read from the terminal.

This chapter describes how the various tasks mentioned above can be performed by user programs. In order to provide a familiar framework on which to base our discussion, we will describe things in terms of *csh* commands. Those readers not familiar with *csh* may wish to read *An Introduction to the C Shell* by William Joy in Section 2c (User's Supplementary Documents) of *The UNIX Programmer's Manual*.

Preliminary Concepts

The Controlling Terminal

When a terminal file (e.g., */dev/tty12*) is opened, it causes the opening process to wait until a connection is established. In practice, user programs rarely open these files directly; they are opened by the *init* process and become a user's standard input and output files. The first terminal file open in a process becomes the *controlling terminal* for that process. The controlling terminal is inherited by a child process during a *fork*, even if the controlling terminal is closed.

The file */dev/tty* is, in each process, a synonym for the controlling terminal associated with that process. It is useful for programs that wish to be sure of writing messages on the terminal no matter how output has been redirected.

Certain processes in the system, usually the daemons started at system boot time, clear their controlling terminal using the `ioctl` system call (with `TIOCNOTTY` as the operation constant). The reasons for this will become apparent later.

Process Groups

On non-Berkeley versions of the UNIX system, the set of processes that share the same controlling terminal is defined as a *process group*. This definition still applies on Berkeley systems when using *sh* and the old tty driver. Because neither of these permits job control, this definition will not be discussed further.

On Berkeley systems, it is possible to place processes into any arbitrary process group using the `setpgrp` system call. The C shell uses this call in a straightforward way; each shell *job* constitutes a single process group. Each time it starts a process, *csh* sets that process's process group to the same number as its process id. In the case of a pipeline, all the processes in the pipeline are placed in the same process group, the process id of the first process forked (which, as it happens, is the last command in the pipeline).

In addition to associating each process with a process group, each terminal is associated with a process group called a *distinguished* process group. Processes that are in a distinguished process group are considered to be in the "foreground," and are permitted to read from the terminal and to receive interrupts generated from the keyboard. Processes not in a distinguished process group are considered to be in the "background." They cannot read from the terminal, and they do not receive interrupts generated from the keyboard.

The process group associated with a terminal may be obtained using the call:

```
ioctl(fd,TIOCGPGRP,&pgrp)
```

where *pgrp* is an integer and *fd* refers to the terminal in question. The terminal's process group may be changed using the `ioctl` system call with `TIOCSPGRP` as the operation constant.

System Calls

In order to write subroutines that mimic those of *csh*, it is necessary to first describe a few of the system calls we will be using. Several of them have been described in detail in previous chapters, and we will only mention them briefly here to describe what we plan to use them for.

ioctl

`ioctl` will be used to initially set the process group of the controlling terminal to the process group of the shell. This is necessary to allow the shell to print prompts, read from the terminal, and accept signals. We will also use `ioctl` to change the process group of the terminal to permit a job in another process group to access it (thus putting the job in the foreground).

setpgrp

The `setpgrp` system call will be used to put each new process into its process group, and also to place the shell into a process group when it is first invoked.

killpg

`killpg` is very similar to `kill`, except that it sends the signal to a process group instead of a single process. This call is used to send signals to the various process groups the shell is controlling.

wait3

This call is a much more sophisticated version of the `wait` system call. It is called as:

```
wait3(status, options, rusage)
```

where *status* is a pointer to type *union wait*; *options* is an integer containing ORed-in bits described below; and *rusage* is an optional pointer to type `struct rusage`. If non-zero, it will be filled in with resource usage statistics about the child process. The union and the options flags are defined in the include file *sys/wait.h*; the other structure is defined in *sys/resource.h*. As with `wait`, the process id of the process whose status is being given is returned, and –1 is returned when there are no processes that wish to report their status. The flags which can be ORed into `options` are:

WNOHANG   This flag specifies that the call should not block if there are no processes which wish to report their status. This enables a process to check for any processes whose status has changed and then go on to something else if there are none.

WUNTRACED   This flag causes children which have been stopped via one of the signals SIGTTIN, SIGTTOU, SIGTSTP, or SIGSTOP to have their status reported also.

There are also three macros defined; each takes a single argument, the `union wait` object:

WIFSTOPPED   Returns non-zero if the process is stopped.

WIFSIGNALED   Returns non-zero if the process exited because of a signal.

WIFEXITED   Returns non-zero if the process exited of its own accord.

The JOB and PROC Data Types

In the following discussion, we will be presenting several subroutines, each of which performs a single task related to job control. To avoid complicating the examples, we have assumed a generic data type called *JOB*. This data type is used to describe each job, and contains such information as the command string, the process group number, the process ids of the processes in the job, and the status of the processes.

Another data type, *PROC*, will be used to represent a single process within a job. Rather than explicitly define these data types, we will simply use fields from them as we need them, and rely on the comments in the code to explain what is being done.

Job Control in the Shell

This section describes the various parts of job control that are handled primarily by the shell. This includes moving processes from foreground to background and back, suspending processes in mid-execution, and so on.

Setting Up for Job Control

In order to perform job control, it is first necessary to set up the environment. This set-up is done by the shell when it is first invoked, and includes setting the shell's process group and then setting the terminal's process group. Example 10-1 shows how this might be done.

Example 10-1. setupjc—set up for job control

```
#include <sys/ioctl.h>

int MyPid;        /* the shell's process id     */
int MyPgrp;       /* the shell's process group  */
int TermPgrp;     /* the terminal's process group */

setup()
{
    /*
     * Obtain shell's process id.
     */
    MyPid = getpid();

    /*
     * Just use pid for process group.  This is
     * not a requirement, just convenient.  Other
     * ways of picking a process group can be used.
     */
    MyPgrp = MyPid;
    TermPgrp = MyPid;

    /*
     * Set the shell's process group.
     */
    if (setpgrp(MyPid, MyPgrp) < 0) {
        perror("setpgrp");
        exit(1);
    }

    /*
     * Set the terminal's process group.
     */
    if (ioctl(1, TIOCSPGRP, &MyPgrp) < 0) {
        perror("ioctl");
        exit(1);
    }
}
```

Executing a Program

When executing a program, the shell performs something similar to what is done in Example 9-2. The actual routine handles more complex things than the example; in particular, the routine is recursive after a fashion in order to handle building pipelines.

The important thing about executing programs, though, is that after the first child has been spawned (the child whose process id will become the process group for this job), the terminal must be placed in this process group. If this is not done, the program will not be executing in the foreground (though, of course, this is what is wanted if the command line contained an ampersand on the end). It is not terribly important whether the parent or the child sets the process group, as long as it gets done. In *csh*, the parent shell handles this.

Stopping a Job

There are two ways to stop a job in *csh*. The first method, using the ''^Z'' or ''^Y'' keys on the terminal, is used to stop the current foreground job and return control to the shell. (^Z stops the process immediately. ^Y does not stop the process until it tries to read from the terminal.) The second method, the `stop` shell command, is used to stop processes that are already in the background.

Stopping a job involves two steps. If the stopped job is already in the background, the process group of the job must be sent a stop signal. If the job is in the foreground, typing the stop character on the keyboard causes the system to send the job the stop signal. If the stopped job was in the foreground, the process group of the terminal must be changed to the process group of the shell, which allows the shell to print its prompt and read the next command. Example 10-2 demonstrates the `stop` subroutine.

Example 10-2. stop—stop a job

```
#include <signal.h>

stop(j)
JOB *j;
{
    /*
     * If the job is already stopped, we don't
     * need to do anything.
     */
    if (j->status & JSTOPPED)
        return;

    /*
```

```
     * If the job's process group is not that of the
     * terminal, then the job is in the background
     * and must be sent a stop signal.
     */
    if (j->pgrp != TermPgrp)
        killpg(j->pgrp, SIGSTOP);

    /*
     * Mark the job as stopped.
     */
    j->status |= JSTOPPED;

    /*
     * If the terminal is not in the shell's process
     * group, we need to put it there.
     */
    if (TermPgrp != MyPgrp) {
        ioctl(1, TIOCSPGRP, &MyPgrp);
        TermPgrp = MyPgrp;
    }
}
```

In this example, we introduced the `status` field of the job structure, which is used to keep track of the status of jobs. Later we will see a similar field used to keep track of the status of each process in a job. The main reason for keeping track of the status of jobs and processes is not for efficiency, but rather *reporting* the status of the jobs to you. This is shown later in this chapter.

Backgrounding a Job

There are two ways to place a job in the background. The first is by placing an ampersand ('&') at the end of the command string when the command is first entered. Since this case is handled when the processes are started, and has little if anything to do with job control, it is not described further here.

The second method, using the `bg` command, involves sending a "continue" signal to the job. Because the job is not in the foreground (otherwise the `bg` command could not have been read by the shell), no process group manipulation is necessary. Example 10-3 shows the `bg` subroutine.

Example 10-3. bg—background a job

```
#include <signal.h>

bg(j)
JOB *j;
{
    /*
     * If the job is already running,
```

```
 * there's no need to start it.
 */
if (j->status & JRUNNING)
    return;

/*
 * Start the job.
 */
killpg(j->pgrp, SIGCONT);

/*
 * Mark the job as running.
 */
j->status &= ~JSTOPPED;
j->status |= JRUNNING;
}
```

Foregrounding a Job

Bringing a job into the foreground is somewhat more complex than putting it into the background. Because the job is not in the process group of the terminal, the terminal's process group must be changed. Secondly, the job must be started if it is in a stopped state. Finally, after the job has been placed into the foreground, the shell must wait for it to complete. This is all shown in Example 10-4.

Example 10-4. fg—foreground a job

```
#include <sys/ioctl.h>
#include <signal.h>

fg(j)
JOB *j;
{
    /*
     * If the terminal is not in the job's process
     * group, change the process group of the
     * terminal.
     */
    if (j->pgrp != TermPgrp) {
        ioctl(1, TIOCSPGRP, &j->pgrp);
        TermPgrp = j->pgrp;
    }

    /*
     * If the job is not running, start it up.
     */
    if (j->status & JSTOPPED) {
        killpg(j->pgrp, SIGCONT);
        j->status &= ~JSTOPPED;
```

```
            j->status |= JRUNNING;
    }

    /*
     * Go wait for the job to complete.
     */
    waitfor();
}
```

The `waitfor` routine is shown in Example 10-5.

The jobs Command

The *jobs* command is used in *csh* to print the status of all running jobs. For the most part, it simply involves running through the data structures for jobs and processes and printing out their status flags. This is contrary to what it *looks* like *jobs* does, since it is reported in the output that each process is running, stopped, finished, etc. However, all the status checking is performed in other parts of the shell, predominantly the `waitfor` routine, discussed next.

Waiting for Jobs

The task of waiting for jobs to complete is somewhat more complex in *csh* than it was when described in Chapter 9, *Executing Programs*. First of all, using `wait3`, not only do we find out about jobs that have exited, but we also find out about those that have changed their status (stopped, etc.). The main problem, however, is decoding all this information and saving it all in the data structures.

The way we do this is as follows: we continue to wait on jobs until either we run out, or the job currently in the foreground changes its status. As we find out about other processes, we OR in various flags into their status fields, and also OR in the constant JNEEDNOTE. Just before we print a prompt, we run through the data structures, and any job that has JNEEDNOTE in its status flags has its status printed out. Example 10-5 shows the `waitfor` routine.

Example 10-5. waitfor—wait for process to finish

```
#include <sys/wait.h>

waitfor()
{
    int pid;
    JOB *j;
    PROC *p;
    JOB *findjob();
    union wait status;
```

```
/*
 * As long as we get something's status back...
 */
while ((pid = wait3(&status, WUNTRACED, 0)) >= 0) {
    /*
     * Find the job structure which has this
     * process.
     */
    j = findjob(pid);

    /*
     * Find the process structure.
     */
    for (p = j->procs; p->pid != pid; p = p->next)
        /* empty */ ;

    /*
     * Find out what happened to the process.
     */
    if (WIFSTOPPED(status)) {
        /*
         * See if we know the reason it was
         * stopped. The w_stopsig element of
         * the structure contains the number
         * of the signal which stopped the
         * process.
         */
        switch (status.w_stopsig) {
        case SIGTTIN:
            p->status |= PTTYINPUT;
            break;
        case SIGTTOU:
            p->status |= PTTYOUTPUT;
            break;
        case SIGSTOP:
            p->status |= PSTOPSIGNAL;
            break;
        default:
            break;
        }

        p->status |= PSTOPPED;
        j->status |= JNEEDNOTE;
    }
    else if (WIFEXITED(status)) {
        /*
         * Normal termination.
         */
        if (status.w_retcode == 0)
            p->status |= PDONE;
        else
            p->status |= PEXITED;
```

```
        p->exitcode = status.w_retcode;

        /*
         * We're only going to note processes
         * exiting if all the processes in the
         * job are complete.
         */
        if (alldone(j))
            j->status |= JNEEDNOTE;
    }
    else if (WIFSIGNALED(status)) {
        p->status |= PSIGNALED;

        /*
         * Save the termination signal.
         */
        p->termsig = status.w_termsig;

        /*
         * Check for a core dump.
         */
        if (status.w_coredump)
            p->status |= PCOREDUMP;

        /*
         * We're only going to note processes
         * exiting if all the processes in the
         * job are complete.
         */
        if (alldone(j))
            j->status |= JNEEDNOTE;
    }

    /*
     * If this process is the one which was in the
     * foreground, we need to do special things,
     * and then return to the main control section
     * of the shell.
     */
    if (j->pgrp == TermPgrp) {
        /*
         * If the job is stopped, we need to call
         * the stop routine.
         */
        if (WIFSTOPPED(status)) {
            stop(j);
            printf("Stopped\n");
        }

        /*
         * If the job exited or died somehow, we
         * need to regain control of the terminal.
         */
```

```
    if (WIFEXITED(status) || WIFSIGNALED(status)) {
        ioctl(1, TIOCSPGRP, &MyPgrp);
        TermPgrp = MyPgrp;
    }

    /*
     * Go back.
     */
    return;
        }
    }
}
```

Asynchronous Process Notification

By using the *notify* command supplied by *csh*, it is possible to find out immediately when the status of a job changes, rather than waiting until the next prompt is printed. The way this is done involves catching the SIGCHLD signal in the parent shell. This signal is sent to a process whenever one of its children changes its status. When no processes require asynchronous notification, this signal is simply ignored.

The routine in *csh* that handles asynchronous notification is simply declared as the handler for the SIGCHLD signal. When it is called, it makes a single call to wait3, since we are guaranteed to have a process there that has changed status. The rest of the routine looks very much like the waitfor routine shown in Example 10-5, except that at the end of the routine a call is made to the routine that prints out the job status fields.

Job Control Outside the Shell

As mentioned previously, processes that are not in the distinguished process group are not permitted to read from the terminal. Under other versions of UNIX, as well as under the old tty driver on Berkeley systems, these processes receive an end-of-file when they attempt to read from the terminal.

Under the new tty driver, however, the process receives a SIGTTIN signal which causes it to stop. The shell can then be used to place the job in the foreground, and the read can be satisfied.

Processes are normally allowed to write to the terminal regardless of whether or not they are in the foreground. Under the new tty driver, if the LTOSTOP bit is set in the local mode word, then processes that are not in the distinguished process group are stopped with a SIGTTOU signal when they attempt to write to the terminal. They can then be moved into the foreground with the shell, at which point they can continue their output. This is particularly convenient for letting long-running programs run in the background until they are ready to print, and then having them wait until you are ready to see the output.

Important Points

There are several important points to notice from this chapter and its examples:

- The examples in this chapter are for demonstration purposes only. They will work well enough as a demonstration, but they would not be suitable for incorporation into a real shell program. In order to do this, it would be necessary to protect several areas of the code from interruption by signals (in particular, since the SIGCHLD handler works on the same data structures as the other routines, SIGCHLD must be ignored when modifying these structures), built-in commands would have to be handled specially, such as interruption of shell procedures (stopping a process which was executed from inside a shell construct such as a *foreach* loop causes the rest of the loop to be aborted), and so on.

- Throughout the examples, whenever a process needed to be placed in the same process group as the terminal, it was always the *terminal* process group that was changed. An alternative method would have been to use setpgrp to change the process group of the process. There is, however, a reason for changing the terminal's process group and not the process's: if the process uses its own process group for something, and obtains that information via getpgrp, then if the shell changes the process's process group that information will no longer be accurate. For this reason, it is always the terminal's process group that is changed.

- In Chapter 9, *Executing Programs*, we mentioned that the shell will ignore SIGINT and SIGQUIT in processes that it places in the background. This is not desirable when in a job control environment, since there is no way, when bringing the job into the foreground, to cause these signals not to be ignored anymore. Fortunately, it is not necessary to ignore these signals in background processes when working with the new tty driver. Recall that signals generated from the keyboard are sent *only* to the processes in the process group of the terminal. Since background processes are not in this process group, they will not receive the signal anyway. However, when they are placed into the foreground, the interrupt keys will work correctly, since the background processes are not ignoring the signals themselves.

- The code shown will not work correctly if the process changes its process group or if something changes the terminal's process group. The C shell correctly handles these cases.

Job control is a very useful feature to have in UNIX systems; unfortunately the implementation is rather complicated. Generally speaking, there is no way to implement "part" of job control, it's an all-or-nothing prospect. Most programs, with the exception of *csh* and the Korn shell (*ksh*), do not handle stopping processes started from them simply because it requires too much code. The actual *csh* implementation of job control, counting only the code to handle manipulation and status printing of processes, requires about 1200 lines of C code.

11

Interprocess Communication

Berkeley UNIX IPC
System V IPC

The interprocess communication (IPC) facilities of the UNIX system allow two or more distinct processes to communicate with each other. We have already discussed one form of IPC, the `pipe`. This mechanism allows two related processes (one of which must be a descendant of the other) to communicate over a two-way byte stream using the `read` and `write` system calls.

The newer versions of UNIX (Berkeley versions starting with 4.2BSD and System V) provide more powerful IPC facilities that allow two or more completely unrelated processes to communicate with each other. System V provides three separate forms of IPC: *semaphores*, *shared memory*, and *message queues*. Each of these mechanisms, while powerful in its own area, tends to be rather restrictive in the types of uses to which it can be put. The Berkeley UNIX method, called *sockets*, provides an interface that is a generalization of the pipe mechanism already familiar to most UNIX programmers. In fact, the pipe mechanism is actually implemented in Berkeley UNIX as a pair of connected sockets. We will discuss the Berkeley UNIX method first since it is the simplest method to understand. After the basic concepts have been covered, the System V mechanisms will be discussed.

Interprocess communication beyond the scope of the pipe mechanism can normally be described using a client/server model. In this model, one process is called the *server*; it is responsible for satisfying requests put to it by the other process, the *client*. As an example, consider a program that manages all the printer queues on a machine. This program would be called a server. When a user prints a file, the printing program (the client) contacts the server and asks it to put the file into the queue for the specified printer. The server does this, and then invokes the appropriate program to actually print the file on the printer.

Normally, when a server program is invoked, it asks the operating system for a socket. When it gets one, it assigns a well-known *name* to that socket, so that other programs can ask the operating system to talk to that name (since they will not know the integer value of the socket itself). After naming the socket, the server listens on the socket for connection requests from client processes to come in. When a connection request arrives, the server may accept or reject the connection. If it accepts the connection, the operating system joins the client and server together at the socket, and the server may read and write data to and from the socket just as if it were a pipe to the client.

The client begins the process by asking the operating system for a socket, and then asking that the socket be connected to some other socket having a given name. The operating system attempts to find a socket with the given name, and if it does, sends the process listening to that socket a connection request. If that process (the server) accepts the connection, the operating system joins the two processes together at the socket, and the client can read and write data to and from the socket just as if it were a pipe to the server.

In the Berkeley UNIX implementation, socket names are simply standard UNIX path names. For example, in the case of the printer software described above, the server might listen on the socket called */dev/printer*. Currently, the IPC mechanism actually creates entries in the file system for these sockets (i.e., you can see them in directories).

The socket System Call

The socket system call is used to obtain a socket descriptor for performing IPC operations. It takes three arguments: a *domain*, a *socket type* and a *protocol*. The various constants used as arguments to the call are defined in the include file *sys/socket.h*; *sys/types.h* must also be included.

The domain argument specifies to the operating system the domain in which addresses should be interpreted. This domain imposes certain rules on address formats and their interpretation. In this chapter, which describes communication between processes on the same computer, we will be using the UNIX domain, in which addresses are interpreted as UNIX path names. This domain is specified to socket using the AF_UNIX constant (the "AF" stands for "address family"). Another important domain, the Internet domain, is discussed in the next chapter. (4.3BSD provides a third domain, the Xerox NS domain. This domain will not be discussed in this book.)

The socket type argument specifies the type of communications channel that should be used with the socket. There are several types of communications channels available with Berkeley UNIX IPC, but only two are of interest to the general user:

SOCK_STREAM   This type of connection is usually called a *virtual circuit*. It is a continuous byte stream that guarantees reliable delivery of data in the order it was sent. No data can be sent until the circuit has been established; the circuit then remains intact until the conversation is complete. A telephone call is a "real world" example of a virtual circuit; a UNIX pipe is also a virtual circuit.

SOCK_DGRAM   This type of connection is used to send distinct packets of information called *datagrams*. Datagrams are not guaranteed to be delivered in order to the remote side; in fact, they are not guaranteed to be delivered at all. (This may sound undesirable, but there are several applications that can make use of datagrams quite well.) The U.S. Mail system is an example of datagrams: letters can arrive out of sequence, and some may even get lost.

The protocol argument allows the programmer to pick which protocol is used to implement the communications channel. If the protocol argument is given as zero, the operating system will pick the correct protocol automatically. All the examples in this book will allow the operating system to choose the protocol.

socket returns an integer file descriptor suitable for use with read and write (after the socket has been connected to something) as well as the other IPC system calls. If the socket cannot be created (having too many files open is one of the reasons this call can fail), −1 is returned and errno is set to the reason for failure.

The bind System Call

The bind system call is used to assign a name to a socket. Until a socket has been given some type of name (naming schemes vary with the addressing domain being used), it cannot be addressed by client programs. bind takes three arguments: the socket to be named (which must have been created with a call to socket), a pointer to the name of the socket, and the length of the name. It returns 0 if the call succeeds; –1 is returned and errno is set if it fails.

The second argument to bind is a structure of the generic type sockaddr. For the UNIX domain, the structure is actually of type sockaddr_un, and is defined in the include file *sys/un.h*. The sockaddr_un structure is defined as follows:

```
struct     sockaddr_un {
    short     sun_family;        /* AF_UNIX    */
    char      sun_path[108];     /* path name */
};
```

The sun_family element is set to AF_UNIX, which indicates the addressing family of the address. sun_path contains the path name of the socket we will be using. As a side effect of the implementation, the file named in sun_path is actually created when it is bound. Because of this, whenever the socket's owner is finished with it it should unlink the socket, or the next program to attempt to bind its name will receive an error that the address is already in use.

The send and recv System Calls

The send and recv system calls are analogous to read and write, except that they may only be used with sockets. (The read and write system calls may also be used on stream sockets; the operating system performs the appropriate translations.) The calls accept identical arguments to read and write, except that there is a fourth argument for specifying special options. Two of these options are:

MSG_PEEK By specifying this option in a call to recv, the program can "peek" at data on the socket without actually "reading" it. That is, although the buffer is filled with the requested data, a subsequent read or recv call will receive the same data again. This is sometimes useful for deciding what to do with received data without having to read it in and deal with it ahead of time.

MSG_OOB This option causes send to send the requested data as *out of band* data. It also allows recv to read data that has been sent out of band. When sending data on a stream connection, the data is transmitted in the order it was written. If an urgent condition arises, there is no way to inform the reading process about it immediately, since the reading process must read and process all the data currently on the socket. Out of band data is sent outside the normal data stream, effectively "jumping over" all the data waiting to be read. When it arrives at the reading process, the process may receive a signal (see Chapter 8, *Processing Signals*), and it can be processed immediately. (This is how the *rlogin* program flushes output when an interrupt is received.)

The listen System Call

The listen call is used by the server to inform the operating system that connection requests on a given socket should be delivered to the program. If no program is listening for connections on the socket, any connection requests to that address will be refused. listen takes two arguments: the socket to listen on and an integer *backlog*. The backlog indicates how many connections can be pending on the socket awaiting acceptance (most systems limit the size of the backlog to five). This enables a program to have more than one program connect to it at once; the operating system will queue up the backlog amount of requests and hand them to the program one at a time. If the server is backed up to the maximum backlog size, incoming connections will still not be refused. Rather, the operating system discards the data packets requesting the connection. The purpose is to allow connections to time out rather than be refused, in order that the client may distinguish between a server that is too busy and a server that is down.

The shutdown System Call

The shutdown call is used to shut down all or part of a connection on a socket. It takes two arguments: the socket to be shut down and an integer indicating how to shut the socket down. If the integer is 0 the socket is shut down for reading; all further reads from the socket return end-of-file. If the number is 1, the socket is shut down for writing; all further writes to the socket fail. If the integer is 2, the socket is shut down for both reading and writing (the connection is effectively terminated).

The close system call may also be used to terminate a connection, with slightly different results. If the protocol being used by the socket guarantees reliable data delivery, a close on the socket will block while the operating system attempts to deliver any data remaining "in transit." The shutdown call, on the other hand, indicates to the operating system that this data is not wanted and no effort to deliver it need be made.

Connection-based Sockets

Sockets of type SOCK_STREAM must be *connected* before they can be used. This connection process establishes the circuit that will be used until the connection is terminated. Two system calls are used to make connections, one by the server and the other by the client.

The accept System Call

The accept system call is used by the server to accept a connection on a socket. The socket must first have been listened on. When accept is called, it will block the process until a connection comes in.* When a connection arrives, accept returns a new socket descriptor that is connected to the client process. This way the server uses the new descriptor to converse with the client, and continues accepting connections on the old socket (the one bound to the well-known address).

accept takes three arguments: the socket to accept connections from, a pointer to a sockaddr structure for the appropriate domain, and a pointer to an integer. The integer should contain the size of the sockaddr structure. The sockaddr structure and the integer will be filled in with the address and address length of the client process when a connection is accepted. This permits a server to determine exactly which client it is talking to. If the server is uninterested in the client's address, the second argument may be given as a null pointer.

The connect System Call

connect is used by the client process to establish a conversation with a server. It takes three arguments: an open socket descriptor, a pointer to a sockaddr structure for the appropriate domain which contains the address to be connected to, and an integer indicating the the length of the address. If the call succeeds, 0 is returned; otherwise, −1 is returned and errno will contain the reason for failure.

Connectionless Sockets

Sockets that use the SOCK_DGRAM method of communication do not need to be connected in order to be used. This is because modified versions of send and recv, sendto and recvfrom, are used to send and receive datagrams.

---

*Unless the socket has had non-blocking I/O set on it; see Chapter 5, *Device I/O Control*.

The sendto System Call

`sendto` takes six arguments. The first four arguments are the same as those for `send`: a socket descriptor, a pointer to a character buffer, the number of bytes to be sent, and a flags word. The last two arguments are a pointer to a structure of type `sockaddr` and an integer indicating the size of the structure. A datagram will be sent to the address specified in the structure. No confirmation of delivery is needed (or given), since datagrams are not guaranteed to be delivered.

The recvfrom System Call

`recvfrom` also takes six arguments. The first four arguments are the same as for `recv`: a socket descriptor, a pointer to a character buffer, the number of bytes to be read, and a flags word. The last two arguments are a pointer to a structure of type `sockaddr` and a pointer to an integer. The integer should initially be set to the size of the structure; on return it will be set to the actual size of the address. When the server issues a call to `recvfrom`, the buffer will be filled in with the data from a datagram sent to the server. Additionally, the structure will be filled in with the address of the process which sent the datagram.

Connecting Datagram Sockets

A client may use the `connect` call to connect a datagram socket to a server. Although this does not actually establish a connection, it enables the client to send datagrams on the socket without specifying the address each time.

A Small Client Program

Example 11-1 shows a small client program that connects to a pre-defined address and then reads and writes a few strings. This program can be used to converse with the server program shown in Example 11-2.

Example 11-1. unix-client—client program to demonstrate UNIX domain sockets

```
#include <sys/types.h>
#include <sys/socket.h>
#include <sys/un.h>
#include <stdio.h>

#define NSTRS       3           /* no. of strings  */
#define ADDRESS     "mysocket"  /* addr to connect */

/*
 * Strings we send to the server.
 */
```

```
char *strs[NSTRS] = {
    "This is the first string from the client.\n",
    "This is the second string from the client.\n",
    "This is the third string from the client.\n"
};

main()
{
    char c;
    FILE *fp;
    register int i, s, len;
    struct sockaddr_un saun;

    /*
     * Get a socket to work with.  This socket will
     * be in the UNIX domain, and will be a
     * stream socket.
     */
    if ((s = socket(AF_UNIX, SOCK_STREAM, 0)) < 0) {
        perror("client: socket");
        exit(1);
    }

    /*
     * Create the address we will be connecting to.
     */
    saun.sun_family = AF_UNIX;
    strcpy(saun.sun_path, ADDRESS);

    /*
     * Try to connect to the address.  For this to
     * succeed, the server must already have bound
     * this address, and must have issued a listen()
     * request.
     *
     * The third argument indicates the "length" of
     * the structure, not just the length of the
     * socket name.
     */
    len = sizeof(saun.sun_family) + strlen(saun.sun_path);

    if (connect(s, &saun, len) < 0) {
        perror("client: connect");
        exit(1);
    }

    /*
     * We'll use stdio for reading
     * the socket.
     */
    fp = fdopen(s, "r");

    /*
```

```
     * First we read some strings from the server
     * and print them out.
     */
    for (i=0; i < NSTRS; i++) {
        while ((c = fgetc(fp)) != EOF) {
            putchar(c);

            if (c == '\n')
                break;
        }
    }

    /*
     * Now we send some strings to the server.
     */
    for (i=0; i < NSTRS; i++)
        send(s, strs[i], strlen(strs[i]), 0);

    /*
     * We can simply use close() to terminate the
     * connection, since we're done with both sides.
     */
    close(s);

    exit(0);
}
```

A Small Server Program

Example 11-2 shows a small server program that converses with the client program in Example 11-1. This program should be started first in the background, and then the client should be executed.

Example 11-2. unix-server—server program to demonstrate doman sockets

```
#include <sys/types.h>
#include <sys/socket.h>
#include <sys/un.h>
#include <stdio.h>

#define NSTRS        3              /* no. of strings  */
#define ADDRESS      "mysocket"    /* addr to connect */

/*
 * Strings we send to the client.
 */
char *strs[NSTRS] = {
```

```
    "This is the first string from the server.\n",
    "This is the second string from the server.\n",
    "This is the third string from the server.\n"
};

main()
{
    char c;
    FILE *fp;
    int fromlen;
    register int i, s, ns, len;
    struct sockaddr_un saun, fsaun;

    /*
     * Get a socket to work with.  This socket will
     * be in the UNIX domain, and will be a
     * stream socket.
     */
    if ((s = socket(AF_UNIX, SOCK_STREAM, 0)) < 0) {
        perror("server: socket");
        exit(1);
    }

    /*
     * Create the address we will be binding to.
     */
    saun.sun_family = AF_UNIX;
    strcpy(saun.sun_path, ADDRESS);

    /*
     * Try to bind the address to the socket.  We
     * unlink the name first so that the bind won't
     * fail.
     *
     * The third argument indicates the "length" of
     * the structure, not just the length of the
     * socket name.
     */
    unlink(ADDRESS);
    len = sizeof(saun.sun_family) + strlen(saun.sun_path);

    if (bind(s, &saun, len) < 0) {
        perror("server: bind");
        exit(1);
    }

    /*
     * Listen on the socket.
     */
    if (listen(s, 5) < 0) {
        perror("server: listen");
        exit(1);
    }
```

```
/*
 * Accept connections.  When we accept one, ns
 * will be connected to the client.  fsaun will
 * contain the address of the client.
 */
if ((ns = accept(s, &fsaun, &fromlen)) < 0) {
    perror("server: accept");
    exit(1);
}

/*
 * We'll use stdio for reading the socket.
 */
fp = fdopen(ns, "r");

/*
 * First we send some strings to the client.
 */
for (i=0; i < NSTRS; i++)
    send(ns, strs[i], strlen(strs[i]), 0);

/*
 * Then we read some strings from the client and
 * print them out.
 */
for (i=0; i < NSTRS; i++) {
    while ((c = fgetc(fp)) != EOF) {
        putchar(c);

        if (c == '\n')
            break;
    }
}

/*
 * We can simply use close() to terminate the
 * connection, since we're done with both sides.
 */
close(s);

exit(0);
}
```

System V IPC

System V IPC has three different forms: message queues, semaphores, and shared memory. None of these forms is as simple and generic as the Berkeley UNIX method, but each has its place.

The three forms have several characteristics in common. In each, the specific data structures used are referred to using a *key* of type key_t. A key is simply a long integer, and serves to name the specific data structure to be used so that more than one program can refer to it. Each program uses this key and a "get" system call to ask the system for an identifier, much like a file descriptor, to use when performing IPC operations.

Each form of IPC has a permissions structure associated with it. This set of permissions includes user and group ownership of the mechanism, as well as permissions similar to file permissions specifying who (owner, group, world) may read and/or write (modify) that mechanism. To obtain and modify the permissions on a specific mechanism (including changing the user or group ownership), a control function is called.

Finally, each form of IPC provides various operation functions so that the IPC mechanism may be used. The message queue operation functions allow messages to be sent and received. The semaphore operation functions allows semaphores to be incremented, decremented, and tested for specific values. The shared memory operation functions allow processes to attach and detach shared memory segments to their address space.

Message Queues

Message queues are a cross between a virtual circuit and datagrams. Distinct message "packets" are exchanged between processes using a queue mechanism so that data arrives in order, but the messages can be received in more or less any order determined by the receiving process(es).

A message queue is defined by a unique identifier called a *queue id*, which is usually a long integer. The queue itself is described by the following structure contained in *sys/msg.h*; *sys/types.h* must also be included.

```
struct msqid_ds {
    struct ipc_perm msg_perm;  /* permissions     */
    struct msg *msg_first;     /* 1st message     */
    struct msg *msg_last;      /* last message    */
    ushort      msg_cbytes;    /* # bytes on q    */
    ushort      msg_qnum;      /* # of msgs on q  */
    ushort      msg_qbytes;    /* max # bytes/q   */
    ushort      msg_lspid;     /* last send proc  */
    ushort      msg_lrpid;     /* last recv proc  */
    time_t      msg_stime;     /* last send time  */
    time_t      msg_rtime;     /* last recv time  */
    time_t      msg_ctime;     /* last chg time   */
};
```

The `ipc_perm` structure defines the permissions on the message queue. It is defined in the include file *sys/ipc.h*:

```
struct ipc_perm {
     ushort    uid;      /* owner's user id    */
     ushort    gid;      /* owner's group id   */
     ushort    cuid;     /* creators' user id  */
     ushort    cgid;     /* creator's group id */
     ushort    mode;     /* access permissions */
     ushort    seq;      /* slot sequence number */
     key_t     key;      /* key (queue name)   */
};
```

The msgget System Call

The `msgget` system call is used to create a new message queue, or to obtain the queue id of an existing message queue. It takes two arguments: a key of type `key_t` specifying the name of the message queue, and an integer flags word. A key value of `IPC_PRIVATE` (zero) indicates that the message queue will be used by this process only; non-zero keys are used for queues which will be used by more than one process. The flags word is used to specify the access permissions on the queue; these correspond exactly to normal UNIX file permissions. Specifying read permission for owner, group, or world allows messages to be received; specifying write permission allows messages to be sent. If the value `IPC_CREAT` is ORed into the flags word, a new message queue will be created with the name contained in the key; otherwise the call will return the queue id of the existing message queue whose name matches the key value. If the call succeeds, a queue id is returned; otherwise −1 is returned and `errno` is set to the reason for failure.

The msgctl System Call

The `msgctl` system call is used to get and modify the attributes of an existing message queue. It takes three arguments: the queue id of the message queue, a command constant, and a pointer to a structure of type `msqid_ds`. The valid command constants, defined in the include file *sys/ipc.h*, are:

`IPC_STAT`   Place a copy of the current information about the message queue into the structure.

`IPC_SET`   Set the user id, group id, and mode of the message queue to the values contained in the `msg_perm` element of the structure.

`IPC_RMID`   Remove the message queue identified by the queue id from the system and destroy the message queue. Any operations in progress on the message queue will fail.

The msgsnd and msgrcv System Calls

The system calls used to send and receive messages on a message queue are msgsnd and msgrcv. msgsnd takes four arguments: a queue id, a pointer to a structure of type msgbuf (see below), an integer indicating the size of the message, and a flags word. msgrcv takes five arguments: a queue id, a pointer to a structure of type msgbuf, an integer indicating the maximum size of the message to be received, an integer message type, and a flags word.

The structure used to form a message is declared as follows:

```
struct msgbuf {
    long    mtype;
    char    *mtext;
};
```

The mtype field may be used by processes using the queue to identify types of messages. This value must be greater than zero. mtext is a pointer to a buffer of any number of bytes; the length of this buffer is passed to the routines.

If the flags word contains the constant IPC_NOWAIT, then the msgsnd call will return a failure code immediately if the message queue is full. Otherwise, the call will block until the queue is empty enough to receive the message. Likewise, msgrcv will return a failure code immediately if no messages of the specified type are available, as opposed to blocking until the requested message arrives.

When receiving messages, the caller must provide a message type argument to msgrcv. If this argument is zero, the first message on the queue will be returned. If it is greater than zero, the first message of that type is returned. If it is less than zero, the first message of a type less than or equal to the absolute value of the specified type is returned.

Example 11-3 shows a server program that creates a message queue and then waits for a message to be sent to it. After it receives the message, the program will respond with a message of its own.

Example 11-3. mq-server—server program to demonstrate message queues

```
#include <sys/types.h>
#include <sys/ipc.h>
#include <sys/msg.h>
#include <stdio.h>

#define MSGSZ     128

/*
 * Declare the message structure.
 */
struct msgbuf {
```

```
        long        mtype;
        char        mtext[MSGSZ];
};

main()
{
        int msqid;
        key_t key;
        struct msgbuf sbuf, rbuf;

        /*
         * Create a message queue with "name" 1234.
         */
        key = 1234;

        /*
         * We want to let everyone read and
         * write on this message queue, hence
         * we use 0666 as the permissions.
         */
        if ((msqid = msgget(key, IPC_CREAT | 0666)) < 0) {
            perror("msgget");
            exit(1);
        }

        /*
         * Receive a message.
         */
        if (msgrcv(msqid, &rbuf, MSGSZ, 0, 0) < 0) {
            perror("msgrcv");
            exit(1);
        }

        /*
         * We send a message of type 2.
         */
        sbuf.mtype = 2;
        sprintf(sbuf.mtext, "I received your message.");

        /*
         * Send an answer.
         */
        if (msgsnd(msqid, &sbuf, strlen(sbuf.mtext) + 1, 0) < 0) {
            perror("msgsnd");
            exit(1);
        }

        exit(0);
}
```

Example 11-4 shows a client process that sends a message to the server, and then waits for a response, and prints it on the screen. Before running this program, start up the server process in the background.

Example 11-4. mq-client—client program to demonstrate message queues

```c
#include <sys/types.h>
#include <sys/ipc.h>
#include <sys/msg.h>
#include <stdio.h>

#define MSGSZ      128

/*
 * Declare the message structure.
 */
struct msgbuf {
    long    mtype;
    char    mtext[MSGSZ];
};

main()
{
    int msqid;
    key_t key;
    struct msgbuf sbuf, rbuf;

    /*
     * Get the message queue id for the
     * "name" 1234, which was created by
     * the server.
     */
    key = 1234;

    if ((msqid = msgget(key, 0666)) < 0) {
        perror("msgget");
        exit(1);
    }

    /*
     * We'll send message type 1, the server
     * will send message type 2.
     */
    sbuf.mtype = 1;
    sprintf(sbuf.mtext, "Did you get this?");

    /*
     * Send a message.
     */
    if (msgsnd(msqid, &sbuf, strlen(sbuf.mtext) + 1, 0) < 0) {
        perror("msgsnd");
        exit(1);
    }

    /*
     * Receive an answer of message type 2.
     */
```

```
if (msgrcv(msqid, &rbuf, MSGSZ, 2, 0) < 0) {
    perror("msgrcv");
    exit(1);
}

/*
 * Print the answer.
 */
printf("%s\n", rbuf.mtext);
exit(0);
}
```

Semaphores

Semaphores are special types of flags used for signalling between two processes. They are typically used to guard "critical sections" of code that modify shared data structures. In general, a section of code is written so that it cannot begin until a given semaphore is equal to a specific value. For example, a program might wait until the semaphore is equal to zero. Then it would set the semaphore to one and perform some actions with a shared data structure, and then reset the semaphore to zero. Other processes, also waiting until the semaphore is equal to zero, are effectively "locked out" from modifying the data structure while it is in use. When the semaphore becomes equal to zero again, the system will allow one of the waiting processes to proceed.*

Semaphores are allocated in sets; each set is defined by a unique *semaphore id*. The semaphores in a semaphore set are numbered consecutively starting from zero. The sets themselves are described by a structure of type semid_ds, declared in the include file *sys/sem.h*; *sys/types.h* must also be included:

```
struct semid_ds {
    struct ipc_perm sem_perm;     /* permissions   */
    struct sem     *sem_base;     /* 1st in set    */
    ushort          sem_nsems;    /* # in set      */
    time_t          sem_otime;    /* last op time  */
    time_t          sem_ctime;    /* last chg time */
};
```

---

*This is a simplified explanation. Semaphores are described in detail in most operating system textbooks.

The semget System Call

The `semget` system call is used to create a new set of semaphores or to obtain the semaphore id of an existing set. It takes three arguments: a key of type `key_t` indicating the numeric name of the semaphore set, the number of semaphores desired, and a flags word. The flags word is used to specify the access permissions on the semaphore set; these correspond exactly to normal UNIX file permissions. Specifying read permission for owner, group, or world allows semaphores to be examined; specifying write permission allows semaphores to be changed. If the value `IPC_CREAT` is ORed into the flags word, a new semaphore set will be created with the name contained in the key; otherwise the call will return the semaphore id of the existing semaphore set whose name matches the key value. The call returns an integer semaphore id on success; –1 is returned on failure and `errno` is set to the reason for failure.

The semctl System Call

The `semctl` system call is used for examining and changing the values of specific semaphores in a semaphore set. It takes four arguments: a semaphore id, the number of the semaphore to examine or change (`semnum`), a command constant, and a variable of type `union semun`, as defined below:

```
union semun {
     int     val;
     struct semid_ds *buf;
     ushort *array;
};
```

The command constants are as follows:

GETVAL	Return the value of the semaphore referred to by `semnum`.
SETVAL	Set the value of the semaphore referred to by `semnum` to `semun.val`.
GETPID	Return the process id of the last process to perform an operation on semaphore `semnum`.
GETNCNT	Return the number of processes waiting for the value of semaphore `semnum` to become greater than its current value.
GETZCNT	Return the number of processes waiting for semaphore `semnum` to become equal to zero.
GETALL	Place the values for all semaphores in the set into the array pointed to by `semun.array`.

SETALL   Set all the semaphores in the set to the values contained in the array pointed to by semun.array.

IPC_STAT   Place a copy of the current information about the semaphore set into the structure pointed to by semun.buf.

IPC_SET   Set the user id, group id, and mode of the semaphore set to the values contained in the sem_perm element of the structure pointed to by semun.buf.

IPC_RMID   Remove the semaphore set identified by the semaphore id from the system and destroy the semaphore set. Any operations in progress on the set will fail.

The semop System Call

The semop system call is used to perform operations on semaphores. It takes three arguments: a semaphore id, a pointer to an array of structures of type struct sembuf, and an integer giving the number of elements in the array. The sembuf structure is declared as follows in the include file *sys/sem.h*; *sys/types.h* must also be included:

```
struct sembuf {
     short     sem_num;     /* semaphore number    */
     short     sem_op;      /* semaphore operation */
     short     sem_flg;     /* operation flags     */
};
```

The structure specifies the number of the semaphore it will be used with, the operation to be performed on that semaphore, and flags to control the operation.

For each sembuf structure in the array, the semaphore identified by sem_num will be modified as follows:

- If sem_op is a negative number, and the value of the semaphore is greater than or equal to its absolute value, the absolute value of sem_op will be subtracted from the value of the semaphore.

- If sem_op is a negative number and its absolute value is greater than the value of the semaphore, the process will block until the value of the semaphore becomes greater than or equal to the absolute value of sem_op. When this occurs, the semaphore value will be decremented by the absolute value of sem_op.

- If sem_op is equal to zero and the value of the semaphore is also zero, the call will return immediately.

- If sem_op is equal to zero and the value of the semaphore is non-zero, the process will block until the value of the semaphore becomes zero.
- If the value of sem_op is greater than zero, the value of sem_op will be added to the value of the semaphore.

If the value IPC_NOWAIT is ORed into the flags word, the process will not block as indicated above, but a failure code will be returned immediately by semop.

Shared Memory

Shared memory provides a method for two or more programs to share a segment of virtual memory and use it as if it were actually part of each program. This is useful, possibly in conjunction with semaphores, for having multiple processes update the same data structures.

A shared memory segment is described by a unique identifier called a *shared memory id*. The shared memory segment itself is described by a structure of type shmid_ds, declared in the include file *sys/shm.h*; *sys/types.h* must also be included:

```
struct shmid_ds {
    struct ipc_perm shm_perm; /* permissions      */
    int    shm_segsz;         /* size of seg      */
    sde_t  shm_seg;           /* seg descriptor   */
    ushort shm_lpid;          /* last shmop       */
    ushort shm_cpid;          /* pid of creator   */
    ushort shm_nattch;        /* cur # attached   */
    ushort shm_cnattch;       /* # in mem attached */
    time_t shm_atime;         /* last shmat time  */
    time_t shm_dtime;         /* last shmdt time  */
    time_t shm_ctime;         /* last chg time    */
};
```

The shmget System Call

A shared memory segment is created or accessed using the shmget system call. It takes three arguments: a key of type key_t specifying the numeric name of the shared memory segment, an integer indicating the desired size in bytes of the segment, and a flags word. A key value of IPC_PRIVATE (zero) indicates that the shared memory segment will be used by this process only (rather pointless); non-zero keys are used for segments which will be used by more than one process. The flags word is used to specify the access permissions on the segment; these correspond exactly to normal UNIX file permissions. Specifying read permission for owner, group, or world allows the memory to be accessed; specifying write permission allows it to be modified. If the value IPC_CREAT is ORed into

143

the flags word, a new shared memory segment will be created with the name contained in the key; otherwise the call will return the shared memory id of the existing segment whose name matches the key value. If the call succeeds, an integer shared memory id is returned; if it fails, –1 is returned and errno is set to the reason for failure.

The shmctl System Call

The shmctl system call is used to examine and modify information about a shared memory segment. It takes three arguments: a shared memory id, a command constant, and a pointer to a structure of type shmid_ds. The command constants are:

IPC_STAT   Place a copy of the current information about the shared memory segment into the structure.

IPC_SET   Set the user id, group id, and mode of the segment to the values contained in the shm_perm element of the structure.

IPC_RMID   Remove the segment identified by the shared memory id from the system and destroy the segment. Any operations in progress on the segment will fail.

The shmat System Call

Before a program can use a shared memory segment, it must first *attach* that segment of memory to itself. This is done using the shmat system call. shmat takes three arguments: a shared memory id, a character pointer, and a flags word. Normally, the character pointer is given as zero; non-zero values may be used for specialized applications. The flags word may contain the constant SHM_RDONLY to indicate that the segment should be treated as read-only; otherwise, the segment will be both readable and writable.

shmat will return a character pointer containing the address to be used when referring to the shared memory segment. If the call fails, the value (char *) –1 will be returned, and errno will contain the reason for failure. Once the memory has been attached, it may be assigned to or referenced just as if it were normal program memory.

The shmdt System Call

When a program is finished with a shared memory segment it may detach it using the shmdt system call. This system call takes a single argument, a pointer as returned by shmat.

Example 11-5 shows a small server program that obtains a shared memory segment, and puts some data into it for a client process to read. It then waits until the first element of the segment is changed by the client, indicating that the segment has been read.

Example 11-5. shm-server—server program to demonstrate shared memory

```
#include <sys/types.h>
#include <sys/ipc.h>
#include <sys/shm.h>
#include <stdio.h>

#define SHMSZ     27

main()
{
    char c;
    int shmid;
    key_t key;
    char *shmat();
    char *shm, *s;

    /*
     * We'll name our shared memory segment
     * "5678".
     */
    key = 5678;

    /*
     * Create the segment.
     */
    if ((shmid = shmget(key, SHMSZ, IPC_CREAT | 0666)) < 0) {
        perror("shmget");
        exit(1);
    }

    /*
     * Now we attach the segment to our data space.
     */
    if ((shm = shmat(shmid, NULL, 0)) == (char *) -1) {
        perror("shmat");
        exit(1);
    }

    /*
     * Now put some things into the memory for the
     * other process to read.
     */
    s = shm;

    for (c = 'a'; c <= 'z'; c++)
        *s++ = c;
```

```
        *s = '\0';

        /*
         * Finally, we wait until the other process
         * changes the first character of our memory
         * to '*', indicating that it has read what
         * we put there.
         */
        while (*shm != '*')
            sleep(1);

        exit(0);
}
```

Example 11-6 shows the client program that reads the shared memory segment and prints it on the screen, and then changes the first element of the segment so that the server can exit. Before running this program, the server process should be started in the background.

Example 11-6. shm-client—client program to demonstrate shared memory

```
#include <sys/types.h>
#include <sys/ipc.h>
#include <sys/shm.h>
#include <stdio.h>

#define SHMSZ     27

main()
{
    int shmid;
    key_t key;
    char *shmat();
    char *shm, *s;

    /*
     * We need to get the segment named
     * "5678", created by the server.
     */
    key = 5678;

    /*
     * Locate the segment.
     */
    if ((shmid = shmget(key, SHMSZ, 0666)) < 0) {
        perror("shmget");
        exit(1);
    }

    /*
     * Now we attach the segment to our data space.
     */
```

```
    if ((shm = shmat(shmid, NULL, 0)) == (char *) -1) {
        perror("shmat");
        exit(1);
    }

    /*
     * Now read what the server put in the memory.
     */
    for (s = shm; *s != '\0'; s++)
        putchar(*s);
    putchar('\n');

    /*
     * Finally, change the first character of the
     * segment to '*', indicating we have read
     * the segment.
     */
    *shm = '*';

    exit(0);
}
```

12

Networking

Addresses
Translating Hostnames Into Network
   Numbers
Obtaining Port Numbers
Network Byte Order
Networking System Calls

Berkeley UNIX provides an extensive facility for interprocess communication between processes on different machines. This is done using the Transmission Control Protocol and Internet Protocol (TCP/IP), as specified by the Defense Advanced Research Projects Agency (DARPA) for use on their international network, the ARPANET. Although the most recent release (Release 3.0) of System V UNIX does provide a networking facility, the Berkeley UNIX facility is in much more widespread use, and is the only facility discussed in this book.

The Berkeley UNIX networking facilities are based on the *socket* mechanism, and work in much the same way as the interprocess communication facility discussed in Chapter 11, *Interprocess Communication*. Rather than using the UNIX domain, however, the networking facilities operate in the Internet domain. (Another networking domain, the Xerox NS domain provided by 4.3BSD, is not discussed here.)

Addresses

In the UNIX domain, the address of a program is specified by using a standard UNIX path name. In the Internet domain, however, this is not viable for two reasons. First, standard path names do not provide any method for specifying which computer a program is located on.* Second, not all the computers connected to a network will necessarily be running the UNIX operating system.

The addresses used in the Internet domain consist of two numbers. The first number is a 32-bit *internetwork number* of the computer which the program to be accessed resides on. Each machine on a network, whether it be the global ARPANET or simply a local-area network, has a unique internetwork number. It should be noted here that although a network number functions as the name of a machine, it is *not* the same thing as the *hostname* of a machine. A hostname is usually a text string (such as "intrepid.ecn.purdue.edu" or "sri-nic.arpa"), and is not easily used as a network address because it does not give any information about how to access the machine itself. Because the same host can reside on more than one network, it is possible for a single hostname to be associated with several network numbers. Each network number specifies to the operating system how to reach the machine by using a different network path.

The second number making up an Internet domain address is a 16-bit *port number*. Each networking program on a machine uses a separate port number; the port number is somewhat similar to the path name used in the UNIX domain. For example, the *rlogin* program uses port number 513, and the FTP file transfer server uses port number 21. Thus, a program wishing to connect to the file transfer server residing on the machine with network number 12345 would specify the Internet address (12345, 21). Without using port numbers, it would be difficult for any machine to run more than one network program at a time. There are other schemes in use besides port numbers, but they will not be discussed here.

Translating Hostnames Into Network Numbers

As mentioned in the previous section, a hostname cannot function as a network address; it must be converted to a network number. The relationships between hostnames and network numbers are stored in the text file /etc/hosts.† To

---

*Some other methods of networking, e.g., Chaosnet, do provide a method for specifying the machine in the path name.

†Actually, many systems now look up addresses dynamically using *name servers*, but this is beyond

translate hostnames into network numbers, the `gethostbyname` library routine is used. This routine takes a single argument, a character string containing the name of the host to be looked up. It returns a pointer to a structure of type `hostent`, as defined in the include file *netdb.h* :

```
struct hostent {
     char    *h_name;         /* name of host   */
     char    **h_aliases;     /* alias list     */
     int     h_addrtype;      /* host addr type */
     int     h_length;        /* length of addr */
     char    **h_addr_list;   /* list of addrs  */
#define    h_addr   h_addr_list[0]
};
```

The `h_addr_list` element of this structure contains all the network numbers associated with the hostname. The `h_addr` "element" is for backward compatibility, but is still often used in programs that don't really care which network number they use to access a machine. If the hostname cannot be found in the database, the constant NULL is returned.

Another library routine, `gethostbyaddr`, exists to look up network numbers and obtain the hostname associated with them. It also returns a pointer to a structure of type `hostent`; the `h_name` field of this structure will contain the hostname.

Obtaining Port Numbers

Most network services (file transfer, remote login, etc.) programs usually use standard "well-known" port numbers—that is, port numbers which are the same everywhere, and are set forth in the specifications of the protocols which use them. This enables a client program on one machine to contact a server program on any other machine without having to guess at what port the server resides. Port numbers for "well-known" services are listed, along with their service names, in the text file */etc/services* .

To obtain the port number for a service, the `getservbyname` library routine is used. This routine takes two arguments: a character string containing the name of the service to be looked up, and a character string usually containing either the value *tcp* or *udp*. The second argument is used to specify whether the program wants the port for a virtual circuit (*tcp*) or a datagram (*udp*) connection.*

---

the scope of this book.

*UDP stands for User Datagram Protocol, and is one of the DARPA protocols.

get servbyname returns a pointer to a structure of type servent, defined in
the include file *netdb.h* :

```
struct servent {
    char    *s_name;       /* service name   */
    char    **s_aliases;   /* alias list     */
    int     s_port;        /* port number    */
    char    *s_proto;      /* protocol to use */
};
```

If the service cannot be found in the database, the constant NULL is returned.

It should be noted that a port does not have to be listed in the database to be used.
Any program may use any port it wants to (provided it's not already in use), with
two exceptions. The ARPANET administration has decreed that port numbers
below 512 are reserved for services which it approves. Further, Berkeley UNIX
imposes the rule that port numbers below 1024 may only be used by the super-
user. Thus, regular user programs are restricted to port numbers between 1025
and 32767. This should be more than enough for a long time to come.

Network Byte Order

Before discussing the system calls used for networking, it is necessary to discuss
the *byte order* of numbers used by the networking software. The method in which
integers are stored in computers varies from vendor to vendor. Some computers
store integers with the most significant bit in the lowest address, while others
store them with the most significant bit in the highest address. Because great
chaos would result if two machines using different byte orders were to try to communicate directly, the network software requires that all data be exchanged in
network byte order .

In order to convert integers to network byte order, two library routines, htons
and htonl, are provided. These convert short and long integers, respectively,
from host byte order to network byte order. Likewise, two other routines, ntohs
and ntohl, exist to convert short and long integers from network byte order to
host byte order.

The gethostbyname and getservbyname routines return all the data in
their structures in network byte order.

Networking System Calls

The system calls used to perform networking tasks are the same system calls used for interprocess communication, described in Chapter 11, *Interprocess Communication*. There are a few differences in the parameters passed to these system calls, however.

- The first parameter to *socket* is now given as AF_INET, which specifies the Internet domain. The second parameter may still be either SOCK_STREAM or SOCK_DGRAM.

- The type of sockaddr structure used with accept, bind, connect, sendto, and recvfrom is now of type sockaddr_in, and is declared in the include file *netinet/in.h* :

```
struct sockaddr_in {
    short       sin_family;
    u_short     sin_port;
    struct in_addr sin_addr;
    char        sin_zero[8];
};
```

- The sin_port element of the structure should contain the port number (in network byte order) to be connected to. The sin_addr element should contain the network number (in network byte order) of the machine the port resides on.

- A new system call, gethostname, can be used to obtain the name of the host the program is running on. This routine takes two arguments: a character string to place the hostname into, and an integer indicating the length of the string.

Examples 12-1 and 12-2 show a small server and client program, respectively. These are the programs from Examples 11-1 and 11-2 in Chapter 11, converted to use the Internet domain. Notice that with the exception of how the address is constructed, the programs are virtually the same.

Example 12-1. inet-client—a client to demonstrate Internet domain sockets

```
/*
 * Connects to the local host at port 1234.
 */
#include <sys/types.h>
#include <sys/socket.h>
#include <netinet/in.h>
#include <netdb.h>
#include <stdio.h>
```

```
#define NSTRS       3      /* no. of strings */

/*
 * Strings we send to the server.
 */
char *strs[NSTRS] = {
    "This is the first string from the client.\n",
    "This is the second string from the client.\n",
    "This is the third string from the client.\n"
};

extern int errno;

main()
{
    char c;
    FILE *fp;
    char hostname[64];
    register int i, s;
    struct hostent *hp;
    struct sockaddr_in sin;

    /*
     * Before we can do anything, we need to know
     * our hostname.
     */
    gethostname(hostname, sizeof(hostname));

    /*
     * Next, we need to look up the network
     * address of our host.
     */
    if ((hp = gethostbyname(hostname)) == NULL) {
        fprintf(stderr, "%s: unknown host.\n", hostname);
        exit(1);
    }

    /*
     * Get a socket to work with.  This socket will
     * be in the Internet domain, and will be a
     * stream socket.
     */
    if ((s = socket(AF_INET, SOCK_STREAM, 0)) < 0) {
        perror("client: socket");
        exit(1);
    }

    /*
     * Create the address we will be connecting to.
     * We use port 1234 but put it into network
     * byte order.  Also, we use bcopy (see Chapter
     * 14) to copy the network number.
     */
```

```
        sin.sin_family = AF_INET;
        sin.sin_port = htons(1234);
        bcopy(hp->h_addr, &sin.sin_addr, hp->h_length);

        /*
         * Try to connect to the address.  For this to
         * succeed, the server must already have bound
         * this address, and must have issued a listen()
         * request.
         */
        if (connect(s, &sin, sizeof(sin)) < 0) {
            perror("client: connect");
            exit(1);
        }

        /*
         * We'll use stdio for reading
         * the socket.
         */
        fp = fdopen(s, "r");

        /*
         * First we read some strings from the server
         * and print them out.
         */
        for (i=0; i < NSTRS; i++) {
            while ((c = fgetc(fp)) != EOF) {
                putchar(c);

                if (c == '\n')
                    break;
            }
        }

        /*
         * Now we send some strings to the server.
         */
        for (i=0; i < NSTRS; i++)
            send(s, strs[i], strlen(strs[i]), 0);


        /*
         * We can simply use close() to terminate the
         * connection, since we're done with both sides.
         */
        close(s);

        exit(0);
}
```

Example 12-2. inet-server—a server to demonstrate Internet domain sockets

```
/*
 * Connects to port 1234 on the local host.
 */
#include <sys/types.h>
#include <sys/socket.h>
#include <netinet/in.h>
#include <netdb.h>
#include <stdio.h>

#define NSTRS      3      /* no. of strings */

/*
 * Strings we send to the client.
 */
char *strs[NSTRS] = {
    "This is the first string from the server.\n",
    "This is the second string from the server.\n",
    "This is the third string from the server.\n"
};

extern int errno;

main()
{
    char c;
    FILE *fp;
    int fromlen;
    char hostname[64];
    struct hostent *hp;
    register int i, s, ns;
    struct sockaddr_in sin, fsin;

    /*
     * Before we can do anything, we need
     * to know our hostname.
     */
    gethostname(hostname, sizeof(hostname));

    /*
     * Now we look up our host to get
     * its network number.
     */
    if ((hp = gethostbyname(hostname)) == NULL) {
        fprintf(stderr, "%s: host unknown.\n", hostname);
        exit(1);
    }

    /*
     * Get a socket to work with.  This socket will
     * be in the Internet domain, and will be a
     * stream socket.
     */
```

```
        */
    if ((s = socket(AF_INET, SOCK_STREAM, 0)) < 0) {
        perror("server: socket");
        exit(1);
    }

    /*
     * Create the address that we will be binding to.
     * We use port 1234 but put it into network
     * byte order.  Also, we use bcopy (see
     * Chapter 14) to copy the network number.
     */
    sin.sin_family = AF_INET;
    sin.sin_port = htons(1234);
    bcopy(hp->h_addr, &sin.sin_addr, hp->h_length);

    /*
     * Try to bind the address to the socket.
     */
    if (bind(s, &sin, sizeof(sin)) < 0) {
        perror("server: bind");
        exit(1);
    }

    /*
     * Listen on the socket.
     */
    if (listen(s, 5) < 0) {
        perror("server: listen");
        exit(1);
    }

    /*
     * Accept connections.  When we accept one, ns
     * will be connected to the client.  fsin will
     * contain the address of the client.
     */
    if ((ns = accept(s, &fsin, &fromlen)) < 0) {
        perror("server: accept");
        exit(1);
    }

    /*
     * We'll use stdio for reading the socket.
     */
    fp = fdopen(ns, "r");

    /*
     * First we send some strings to the client.
     */
    for (i=0; i < NSTRS; i++)
        send(ns, strs[i], strlen(strs[i]), 0);
```

```
/*
 * Then we read some strings from the client
 * and print them out.
 */
for (i=0; i < NSTRS; i++) {
    while ((c = fgetc(fp)) != EOF) {
        putchar(c);

        if (c == '\n')
            break;
    }
}

/*
 * We can simply use close() to terminate the
 * connection, since we're done with both sides.
 */
close(s);

exit(0);
}
```

Example 12-3 shows a slightly different program, and also demonstrates the use of datagrams. This program connects to the *daytime* service on each machine named on its command line. *daytime* is a service supported by most hosts on the ARPANET and simply returns the current date and time on the host. There is one bug in this example; if the returned datagram for some reason does not arrive, the program will hang. Normally, a timeout routine (see Chapter 8, *Processing Signals*) would be placed around the call to recvfrom to prevent this.

Example 12-3. daytime—contact the "daytime" datagram service

```
#include <sys/types.h>
#include <sys/socket.h>
#include <netinet/in.h>
#include <netdb.h>
#include <stdio.h>

#define BUFSZ       256
#define SERVICE     "daytime"

main(argc, argv)
int argc;
char **argv;
{
    int s, n, len;
    char buf[BUFSZ];
    struct hostent *hp;
    struct servent *sp;
    struct sockaddr_in sin;

    /*
```

```
 * Get a datagram socket in the Internet
 * domain.
 */
if ((s = socket(AF_INET, SOCK_DGRAM, 0)) < 0) {
    perror("socket");
    exit(1);
}

/*
 * Look up the port number of the service.
 */
if ((sp = getservbyname(SERVICE, "udp")) == NULL) {
    fprintf(stderr, "%s/udp: unknown service.\n", SERVICE);
    exit(1);
}

/*
 * For each host on the command line...
 */
while (--argc) {
    /*
     * Look up the network number of
     * the host.
     */
    if ((hp = gethostbyname(*++argv)) == NULL) {
        fprintf(stderr, "%s: host unknown.\n", *argv);
        continue;
    }

    /*
     * Build the address of the server on
     * the remote machine.
     */
    sin.sin_family = AF_INET;
    sin.sin_port = sp->s_port;
    bcopy(hp->h_addr, &sin.sin_addr, hp->h_length);

    /*
     * Print the name of the host.
     */
    printf("%s: ", *argv);
    fflush(stdout);

    /*
     * Send a datagram to the server.
     */
    if (sendto(s, buf, BUFSZ, 0, &sin, sizeof(sin)) < 0) {
        perror("sendto");
        continue;
    }

    /*
     * Receive a datagram back.
```

```
         */
        len = sizeof(sin);
        n = recvfrom(s, buf, sizeof(buf), 0, &sin, &len);

        if (n < 0) {
            perror("recvfrom");
            continue;
        }

        /*
         * Print the datagram.
         */
        buf[n] = '\0';
        printf("%s\n", buf);
    }

    close(s);
    exit(0);
}
```

13

The File System

Disk Terminology
The "Standard" UNIX File System
The Berkeley Fast File System
Reading Data Blocks From the File System

Every so often, the need arises to gather a large amount of information about all the files contained in a single file system. For example, many sites perform disk space accounting, billing each user for the amount of space he is using on the disk. One method of gathering this information is to read the top-level directory (the file system mount point), and then recurse down through all subdirectories of that directory, and then down through all subdirectories of those directories, and so on. Unfortunately, this method is extremely slow—it requires a lot of operating system overhead to determine the type of each directory entry (file, directory, symbolic link, etc.) and to open each and every directory in the file system.

For this reason, it is usually best to gather the information by reading it directly from the disk without going through the file system. This involves deciphering the data structures stored on the disk that keep track of the file system, as well as sometimes reading the actual data blocks of the files stored in the file system. This chapter provides an introduction to the techniques used for doing exactly that.

Disk Terminology

Before describing how the file system is laid out on the disk, it is necessary to define several terms used when discussing disk drives. Without an understanding of these terms, the rest of this chapter will be meaningless.

A disk drive is usually made up of two parts: (1) the disk pack, on which the actual data is stored, and (2) the hardware used to transfer the data to and from the disk pack. A disk pack is made up of several platters, which are similar to phonograph records, stacked one on top of the other with gaps in between. There are usually about six platters per disk pack, although this number can vary. Each platter has two surfaces on which information can be recorded; the outer surfaces of the top and bottom platters are not used. This provides (for a six-platter pack) ten surfaces on which data can be stored.

There is one read/write head for each surface in the disk pack. The heads can move in and out from the edge to the center of the pack; normally all heads in the disk drive will move as a unit. During a read/write operation, the heads are held stationary over a given section of the platters while the disk pack itself rotates at high speed (typically 3000-4000 rpm). The area that can be read from or written onto by any single stationary head is called a *track*. Tracks are thus concentric circles, and each time the platters complete a revolution an entire track passes under each read/write head. There may be from 100 to 1000 tracks on each surface of a platter. The collection of tracks simultaneously under a read/write head on the surfaces of all the platters is called a *cylinder*. For a six-platter disk pack, each cylinder is made up of ten individual tracks, one from each storage surface. Tracks are divided into smaller units, called *sectors*. A sector is the smallest addressable segment of a track.

Information is recorded on the tracks of a disk surface in *blocks*. In order to use a disk, one must specify the track or cylinder number, the sector number which is the start of the block, and also the surface (head) number. The read/write head assembly is first positioned to the right cylinder. Before reading or writing can begin, the unit has to wait until the appropriate sector comes under the read/write head. Once this happens, the input/output can take place. Thus, there are three factors affecting the disk's input/output speed: (1) *seek time*, the amount of time required to position the read/write heads at the correct cylinder, (2) *latency time*, the amount of time the disk has to wait for the right sector to arrive under the heads, and (3) *transfer time*, the amount of time required to transfer the data to/from the disk.

The specifications for the Fujitsu M2351 "Eagle" and M2361 "Super Eagle" disks, two of the more common disks in use in the UNIX community, are shown below. These drives use two heads per surface instead of one.

Table 13-1: Disk Specifications for Two Common Disks

	Eagle	**Super Eagle**
Unformatted Capacity		
Drive (MB)	474.2	689.8
Track (KB)	28,160	40,960
Disk Platters		
Diameter (inches)	10.5	10.5
Number	6	6
Heads		
Drive	20	20
Surface	2	2
Rotational Speed (RPM)	3,961	3,600
Cylinders	842	842
Transfer Rate (MB/sec)	1.859	2.458
Latency (ms)	7.5	8.33
Seek Time (ms)		
Maximum	35	35
Average	18	18
Minimum	5	5.5

The "Standard" UNIX File System

There are two principal file systems in use with UNIX: the "standard" file system, which has existed since UNIX came into being and is used by Version 7, 4.0 and 4.1BSD, and by System V, and the Berkeley Fast File System, which is used by 4.2 and 4.3BSD. Because it is simpler to understand, the standard file system is described first.*

---

*The block sizes and data structure sizes of the standard file system vary slightly between different versions of UNIX. The implementation described here is that of System V.

In the standard file system developed at Bell Laboratories, each disk drive is divided into one or more partitions, each of which can contain a file system. A file system never spans multiple partitions. The file system is described by its *super-block*, which is a data structure kept at the "front" of the file system. The super-block contains the basic parameters of the file system such as the number of data blocks in the file system, the maximum number of files (i-nodes), and a pointer to the *free list*, a linked list of all the free data blocks in the file system.

Within the file system are files. Some files are special, and are distinguished as directories. These directories contain pointers to other files, some of which may themselves be directories. Associated with each file in the file system is a descriptive structure called an *i-node*. As described in Chapter 4, *Files and Directories*, the i-node contains information such as the size of the file, the owner of the file, its last modification time, and so on. An array of indices that point to the data blocks of the file is also maintained in the i-node. This array is usually made up of from 8 to 16 elements. The first $n-3$ elements contain the addresses of the first $n-3$ data blocks of the file. The next element contains the address of a data block that contains nothing but the addresses of more data blocks. This is called a *singly indirect* block. The next to last element contains the address of a *doubly indirect* block, in which each address is the address of a block of singly indirect addresses. The last element of the array contains the address of a *triply indirect* block, which contains the addresses of doubly indirect blocks. In a file system with a block size of 1024 bytes, there are 256 addresses in a singly indirect block, a doubly indirect block contains the addresses of 256 singly indirect blocks, and a triply indirect block contains the addresses of 256 doubly indirect blocks.*

Following the super-block on the disk, one i-node structure for each possible file in the file system is stored on the disk; typically, several i-nodes are stored in each file system block. After the i-node area, the rest of the disk partition is used for file data blocks. The super-block is described by a structure of type `filsys`, defined in the include file *sys/filsys.h*. Several other files must also be included; these will be shown in Example 13-1:

```
struct filsys {
    ushort   s_isize;           /* i-list size in blocks */
    daddr_t  s_fsize;           /* volume size in blocks */
    short    s_nfree;           /* no. addrs in s_free   */
    daddr_t  s_free[NICFREE];   /* free block list       */
    short    s_ninode;          /* no. i-nodes in s_inode*/
    ushort   s_inode[NICINOD];  /* free i-node list      */
    char     s_flock;           /* lock: free list in use*/
```

---

*Although the data structures provide for triply indirect blocks, all current versions of UNIX only implement up through double indirection. As disk capacities increase, triple indirection may finally become necessary.

```
        char     s_ilock;         /* lock: i-list in use    */
        char     s_fmod;          /* modified flag          */
        char     s_ronly;         /* mounted read-only      */
        time_t   s_time;          /* last s-block update    */
        short    s_dinfo[4];      /* device information     */
        daddr_t  s_tfree;         /* total free blocks      */
        ushort   s_tinode;        /* total free i-nodes     */
        char     s_fname[6];      /* file system name       */
        char     s_fpack[6];      /* file system pack name  */
        long     s_fill[12];      /* spare, unused          */
        long     s_state;         /* file system state      */
        long     s_magic;         /* magic number           */
        long     s_type;          /* type of file system    */
    };
```

Most of this information is not needed by programs reading the disk directly; it is only used by the operating system. The on-disk i-node structure is called dinode, and is defined in the include file *sys/ino.h* :

```
    struct dinode {
        ushort   di_mode;       /* mode and type of file    */
        short    di_nlink;      /* number of links to file  */
        ushort   di_uid;        /* owner's user id          */
        ushort   di_gid;        /* owner's group id         */
        off_t    di_size;       /* number of bytes in file  */
        char     di_addr[40];   /* disk block addresses     */
        time_t   di_atime;      /* time last accessed       */
        time_t   di_mtime;      /* time last modified       */
        time_t   di_ctime;      /* time i-node last changed */
    };
```

As mentioned previously, one of the reasons to read the raw file system structure rather than going through the operating system is to calculate disk space usage. Example 13-1 shows a small program that does exactly this. It takes a single argument, the name of a character-special device that a file system is mounted on. This is usually called the "raw" device, and its name usually starts with an 'r', as in */dev/rdk0c* . This program is for System V file systems; if you are using Version 7, 4.0 or 4.1BSD you will need to make some minor modifications.

Example 13-1. sumdisk-sysv—summarize the disk usage for System V systems

```
    /*
     * Reads the i-node structures from a raw disk
     * device and then sums up the disk usage for
     * each user.  Prints out the number of blocks
     * each user is using.
     */
    #include <sys/sysmacros.h>
    #include <sys/types.h>
    #include <sys/param.h>
    #include <sys/filsys.h>
```

```
#include <sys/inode.h>
#include <sys/ino.h>
#include <fcntl.h>
#include <stdio.h>
#include <pwd.h>

/*
 * Maximum user id.
 */
#ifndef MAXUID
#define MAXUID     32768
#endif

#define SBSIZE    BSIZE                  /* size of super-block   */
#define sblock    sb_un.u_sblock

/*
 * The super-block.  We allow enough room for
 * a complete disk block.
 */
union {
     char    dummy[SBSIZE];
     struct  filsys u_sblock;
} sb_un;

int     nfiles;                          /* no. of files in filsys */

char    *pname;                          /* program name (argv[0]) */
char    *device;                         /* name of disk device    */
char    *filsys;                         /* name of file system    */

size_t blocks[MAXUID];                   /* count of blocks used   */
struct dinode *dinode;                   /* will hold the i-nodes  */

main(argc, argv)
int argc;
char **argv;
{
     int i, fd;
     register ino_t ino;
     register struct dinode *di;

     /*
      * Save the program name and check our arguments.
      */
     pname = *argv;

     if (argc != 2) {
         fprintf(stderr, "Usage: %s raw-disk-device\n", pname);
         exit(1);
     }

     /*
```

```
 * Open the device for reading.
 */
device = *++argv;

if ((fd = open(device, O_RDONLY)) < 0) {
    perror(device);
    exit(1);
}

/*
 * Get the super-block from the device.
 */
getsblock(fd);

/*
 * Get the i-node structures from the device.
 */
getinodes(fd);

close(fd);

/*
 * Zero the block counts.
 */
for (i=0; i < MAXUID; i++)
    blocks[i] = 0;

/*
 * Add up the number of blocks being used by each
 * user id.
 */
for (ino=0; ino < nfiles; ino++) {
    /*
     * ROOTINO is the first i-node; skip any
     * before it.
     */
    if (ino < ROOTINO)
        continue;

    di = &dinode[ino];

    /*
     * If this is zero, the i-node is free (not
     * in use).
     */
    if ((di->di_mode & IFMT) == 0)
        continue;

    /*
     * Count the number of blocks being used by
     * this file. We round the number of bytes to
     * the next highest multiple of 512.
     */
```

```
            if (di->di_uid < MAXUID)
                blocks[di->di_uid] += (di->di_size + 511) / 512;
    }

    /*
     * Print out what we added up.
     */
    printusage();
    exit(0);
}

/*
 * getsblock--get the super-block from the device referred
 *            to by fd.
 */
getsblock(fd)
int fd;
{
    /*
     * Make sure the disk information is current.  This
     * causes all disk writes to be scheduled.
     */
    sync();
    /*
     * Read in the super-block.  It is stored at file
     * system address SUPERBOFF.
     */
    lseek(fd, (long) SUPERBOFF, 0);
    read(fd, (char *) &sblock, SBSIZE);

    /*
     * The number of files (i-nodes) is calculated by
     * multiplying the number of blocks used to hold
     * i-nodes by the number of i-nodes in a block.
     */
    nfiles = sblock.s_isize * INOPB;

    /*
     * Save the name of the file system.
     */
    filsys = sblock.s_fname;
}

/*
 * getinodes--read in the i-node structures from the device
 *            referred to by fd.
 */
getinodes(fd)
int fd;
{
    register ino_t ino;
    register daddr_t iblk;
    struct dinode *malloc();
```

```
    /*
     * Allocate space for them all.
     */
    dinode = malloc(nfiles * sizeof(struct dinode));

    if (dinode == NULL) {
        fprintf(stderr, "%s: out of memory.\n", pname);
        exit(1);
    }

    /*
     * We read in i-nodes a disk block-full at a time.
     * The INOPB constant is the number of i-nodes in
     * a block.
     */
    for (ino = 0; ino < nfiles; ino += INOPB) {
        /*
         * The i-node's disk block number is given by
         * the itod macro.
         */
        iblk = itod(ino);

        /*
         * Read in this block of i-nodes.
         */
        bread(fd, iblk, (char *) &dinode[ino], BSIZE);
    }
}

/*
 * bread--read cnt bytes from fd into buf, starting at
 *          address bno.
 */
bread(fd, bno, buf, cnt)
daddr_t bno;
char *buf;
int cnt;
{
    int n;

    /*
     * Seek to the proper block.  The shifting by BSHIFT
     * converts the block number to a byte address.
     */
    lseek(fd, (long) bno << BSHIFT, 0);

    /*
     * Read in the data.
     */
    if ((n = read(fd, buf, cnt)) != cnt) {
        perror(filsys);
        exit(1);
    }
```

```
}

/*
 * printusage--print out the disk usage in blocks.
 */
printusage()
{
    register int i;
    struct passwd *pwd;
    struct passwd *getpwuid();

    printf("%s (%s):\n", device, filsys);
    printf(" Blocks \t  User\n");

    for (i=0; i < MAXUID; i++) {
        if (blocks[i] == 0)
            continue;

        /*
         * Look up the login name, and use it if
         * we find it.
         */
        if ((pwd = getpwuid(i)) != NULL)
            printf("%8d\t%s\n", blocks[i], pwd->pw_name);
        else
            printf("%8d\t#%d\n", blocks[i], i);
    }
}
```

The program begins by opening the raw disk device as an ordinary file. Recall that in UNIX a device is accessed exactly as an ordinary file would be; and is treated simply as a stream of bytes. The first thing the program needs is the file system's super-block; this is accessed by the getsblock routine, which uses lseek to seek to the start of the super-block (SUPERBOFF), and then reads it in. The number of files is determined by multiplying the number of blocks used to store i-nodes, sblock.s_isize, by the number of i-nodes stored per block, INOPB.

The getinodes routine is used to read in the i-node structures from disk. This is done by allocating memory for all the i-nodes, and then reading them in from disk a block at a time. The itod macro converts an i-node number to the disk address of that i-node, and the bread function reads in data given a disk address.

Once the i-nodes have been read in, it is necessary only to move through the array and tally the blocks in use for each file by user id. If the ANDing of the di_mode element of the structure with the constant IFMT is 0, the i-node is not in use and can be skipped. Finally, the printusage routine is used to print out how much space each user is taking up.

As you may have noticed, the term "block" is used in various contexts and takes on several different meanings. Technically, a block is usually considered to be 512 bytes. Most disk drives use this as their physical block size, meaning that a single disk block takes up 512 bytes. Under Version 7 UNIX, the file system block size was also 512 bytes. Larger "blocks" are typically described in units of 1024 bytes, or kbytes (short for kilobyte).

In 4.0BSD and System V, the *file system* block size was increased to 1024 bytes, or one kbyte. The *disk* block size remained 512 bytes (this is a hardware parameter), but now each file system block referred to two disk blocks, instead of the previous one-to-one correspondence. There are two advantages to this increase. First, the system can access data faster, since it now transfers 1024 bytes at a time instead of 512. Second, larger files can be stored, since each block address now corresponds to twice the number of bytes. Later releases of System V now also provide a 2 kbyte file system block size; this has similar advantages over the 1 kbyte block size. However, as we shall see in the next section, increasing the file system block size without taking other factors into account can cause problems.

The Berkeley Fast File System

In 4.2BSD, Berkeley worked to redesign the UNIX file system to improve its performance. The internal organization of the file system is quite different from that of the standard UNIX file system, but the user interface to the file system was left unchanged. The result of this effort was the Berkeley Fast File System, which we will simply call the new file system.

As with the standard file system, the new file system is described by the super-block. The super-block in the new file system contains much more information than it did before, and because much of this information is critical, the super-block is replicated in several places on the disk to prevent catastrophic loss.

Because the maximum file size in the new file system is 2^{32} bytes, the minimum file system block size is 4096 bytes (4 kbytes). This allows the file's data blocks to still be addressed using only two levels of indirection (the indirect blocks). File systems may have any block size that is a multiple of 4096 bytes; a typical size is 8192 (8 kbytes). The block size is stored in the super-block, allowing different file systems to use different block sizes, something that cannot be done with the standard file system.

The new file system divides its disk partition into several smaller areas called *cylinder groups*. Each cylinder group is made up of one or more consecutive cylinders on the disk, and contains some bookkeeping information, a redundant copy of the super-block, space for i-nodes, and information about the data block allocation in the cylinder group. It is important to note two things here. First, i-nodes are now spread out over the disk, some in each cylinder group, whereas in the standard file system they are all stored together. Second, the information about free data blocks is now stored in each cylinder group, replacing the standard file system's free list.

As mentioned previously, increasing the file system block size eventually begins to cause problems. The reason for this is that under the standard file system, the smallest storage unit is a file system block. Thus, if the block size is 4096, even a file containing only one byte will use up 4096 bytes on the disk. Since most of the data stored in a typical file system consists of small files, the amount of disk space wasted by having a large block size is extreme. Berkeley's calculations show that using the standard file system, a block size of 512 bytes wastes 6.9% of the disk, a block size of 1024 bytes wastes 11.8%, a 2048 byte block size wastes 22.4%, and a 4096 byte block size wastes an unacceptable 45.6% of the disk!

The new file system provides a solution to this problem by allowing each file system block to be further subdivided into one or more *fragments*. Each block can be broken into 2, 4, or 8 fragments, each of which is individually addressable. Consecutive fragments within the same block may be assigned to a single file. Thus, a file which contains 4097 bytes might utilize one file system block of 4096 bytes and one fragment of 1024 bytes. This leaves the other three fragments of the fragmented block available to some other file. The amount of disk space wasted by this scheme is now the same as that for the standard file system with 1024 byte blocks (assuming 1024 byte fragments), or 11.8%. There are several other changes made in the new file system which are beyond the scope of this book. They are described in detail in the paper *A Fast File System for UNIX*, by Marshall Kirk McKusick, William N. Joy, Samuel J. Leffler, and Robert S. Fabry.

The super-block for the Berkeley fast file system is a structure of type `fs`, and is defined in the include file *sys/fs.h*:

```
struct fs {
    struct  fs *fs_link;    /* linked list of file sys */
    struct  fs *fs_rlink;   /* incore super-blocks      */
    daddr_t fs_sblkno;      /* addr of super-block      */
    daddr_t fs_cblkno;      /* offset of cyl-block      */
    daddr_t fs_iblkno;      /* offset of inode-blocks   */
    daddr_t fs_dblkno;      /* first data after cg      */
    long    fs_cgoffset;    /* cylinder group offset    */
    long    fs_cgmask;      /* used to calc fs_ntrak    */
    time_t  fs_time;        /* last time written        */
    long    fs_size;        /* no. of blocks in fs      */
    long    fs_dsize;       /* no. of data blocks in fs*/
    long    fs_ncg;         /* no. of cylinder groups   */
    long    fs_bsize;       /* size of blocks in fs     */
    long    fs_fsize;       /* size of frags in fs      */
```

```
        long    fs_frag;        /* number of frags/block   */
/* these are configuration parameters                      */
        long    fs_minfree;     /* minimum % free blocks   */
        long    fs_rotdelay;    /* ms for optimal next blk */
        long    fs_rps;         /* disk revs per second    */
/* these fields can be computed from the others            */
        long    fs_bmask;       /* calc of blk offsets      */
        long    fs_fmask;       /* calc of frag offsets     */
        long    fs_bshift;      /* calc of logical blkno    */
        long    fs_fshift;      /* calc number of frags     */
/* these are configuration parameters                      */
        long    fs_maxcontig;   /* max no. contiguous blks */
        long    fs_maxbpg;      /* max no. blks/cyl group  */
/* these fields can be computed from the others            */
        long    fs_fragshift;   /* block to frag shift      */
        long    fs_fsbtodb;     /* for fsbtodb and dbtofsb */
        long    fs_sbsize;      /* actual size of super blk*/
        long    fs_csmask;      /* csum block offset        */
        long    fs_csshift;     /* csum block number        */
        long    fs_nindir;      /* value of NINDIR          */
        long    fs_inopb;       /* value of INOPB           */
        long    fs_nspf;        /* value of NSPF            */
        long    fs_optim;       /* optimization preference */
        long    fs_sparecon[5]; /* reserved for future use */
/* sizes det. by number of cyl groups and their sizes      */
        daddr_t fs_csaddr;      /* blk addr cyl grp sum     */
        long    fs_cssize;      /* size of cyl grp sum      */
        long    fs_cgsize;      /* cylinder group size      */
/* these fields should be derived from the hardware        */
        long    fs_ntrak;       /* tracks per cylinder      */
        long    fs_nsect;       /* sectors per track        */
        long    fs_spc;         /* sectors per cylinder     */
/* this comes from the disk driver partitioning            */
        long    fs_ncyl;        /* cylinders in file system*/
/* these fields can be computed from the others            */
        long    fs_cpg;         /* cylinders per group      */
        long    fs_ipg;         /* i-nodes per group        */
        long    fs_fpg;         /* blocks/group * fs_frag  */
/* this data must be re-computed after crashes             */
        struct  csum fs_cstotal; /* cylinder summary info */
/* these fields are cleared at mount time                  */
        char    fs_fmod;        /* super-block modified     */
        char    fs_clean;       /* file system is clean     */
        char    fs_ronly;       /* mounted read-only flag  */
        char    fs_flags;       /* currently unused flag   */
        char    fs_fsmnt[MAXMNTLEN]; /* name mounted on    */
/* these fields retain the current blk allocation info*/
        long    fs_cgrotor;     /* last cg searched         */
        struct  csum *fs_csp[MAXCSBUFS]; /* list of fs_cs */
        long    fs_cpc;         /* cyl per cycle in postbl */
        short   fs_postbl[MAXCPG][NRPOS]; /* head of blks */
        long    fs_magic;       /* magic number            */
```

```
        u_char  fs_rotbl[1];    /* list of blks each rot   */
/* actually longer */
};
```

As with the standard super-block, most of the fields in this structure are only used by the operating system; the average program can ignore them. The on-disk i-node structure is again of type `dinode`, but differs slightly from the standard file system version. It is defined in the include file *sys/inode.h* :

```
struct icommon {
    u_short ic_mode;            /* mode and type of file   */
    short   ic_nlink;           /* number of links to file */
    uid_t   ic_uid;             /* owner's user id         */
    gid_t   ic_gid;             /* owner's group id        */
    quad    ic_size;            /* number of bytes in file */
    time_t  ic_atime;           /* time last accessed      */
    long    ic_atspare;
    time_t  ic_mtime;           /* time last modified      */
    long    ic_mtspare;
    time_t  ic_ctime;           /* last time i-node changed*/
    long    ic_ctspare;
    daddr_t ic_db[NDADDR];      /* disk block addresses    */
    daddr_t ic_ib[NIADDR];      /* indirect blocks         */
    long    ic_flags;           /* status, unused          */
    long    ic_blocks;          /* blocks actually held    */
    long    ic_spare[5];        /* reserved,  unused       */
};

struct dinode {
    union {
        struct  icommon di_icom;
        char    di_size[128];
    } di_un;
};
```

There are constants defined to allow the various fields of the `dinode` structure to be referred to as di_*whatever* as in the fashion of the standard file system. Probably the most important differences between this structure and the one used by the standard file system are first that the direct and indirect block addresses are now stored in separate arrays, and second the addition of the `di_blocks` element. The `di_blocks` element of the structure contains the actual number of blocks used by the file. The reason this is necessary is that files can contain "holes" created by seeking to a large address and then writing data. These holes will be reflected in the `di_size` field of the structure even though they don't actually take up any disk space.

Example 13-2 shows the program from Example 13-1 modified to use the Berkeley Fast File System. If you are using a version of UNIX that uses Sun's Network File System (NFS), be sure to define the constant NFS when compiling this example. This is necessary to access the new data structures introduced by Sun.

Example 13-2. sumdisk-bsd—summarize the disk usage for Berkeley systems

```
/*
 * Reads the i-node structures from a raw disk device and
 * then sums up the disk usage for each user.  Prints out
 * the number of blocks each user is using.
 *
 * If you are on a Sun workstation or other system using Sun's
 * Network File System (NFS), be sure to define the constant
 * NFS so that the proper files get included.
 */

#ifdef sun
#define NFS      1
#endif

#ifdef NFS
#include <sys/param.h>
#include <sys/time.h>
#include <sys/vnode.h>
#include <ufs/inode.h>
#include <sys/file.h>
#include <ufs/fs.h>
#include <stdio.h>
#include <pwd.h>
#else
#include <sys/param.h>
#include <sys/inode.h>
#include <sys/file.h>
#include <sys/fs.h>
#include <stdio.h>
#include <pwd.h>
#endif

/*
 * Maximum user id.
 */
#ifndef MAXUID
#define MAXUID  32768
#endif

#define sblock  sb_un.u_sblock

/*
 * The super block.  We allow enough room for
 * a complete disk block.
 */
union {
    struct   fs u_sblock;
    char     dummy[SBSIZE];
} sb_un;

int nfiles;                 /* number of files in file system      */
```

```
char    *pname;        /* program name (argv[0])             */
char    *device;       /* name of the disk device given      */
char    *filsys;       /* name of the file system on device  */

size_t blocks[MAXUID]; /* count of blocks used               */
struct dinode *dinode; /* will hold all the i-node structures */

main(argc, argv)
int argc;
char **argv;
{
    int i, fd;
    register ino_t ino;
    register struct dinode *di;

    /*
     * Save the program name and check our arguments.
     */
    pname = *argv;

    if (argc != 2) {
        fprintf(stderr, "Usage: %s raw-disk-device\n", pname);
        exit(1);
    }

    /*
     * Open the device for reading.
     */
    device = *++argv;

    if ((fd = open(device, O_RDONLY)) < 0) {
        perror(device);
        exit(1);
    }

    /*
     * Get the super-block from the device.
     */
    getsblock(fd);

    /*
     * Get the i-node structures from the device.
     */
    getinodes(fd);
    close(fd);

    /*
     * Zero the block counts.
     */
    for (i=0; i < MAXUID; i++)
        blocks[i] = 0;

    /*
```

```
     * Add up the number of blocks being used by
     * each user id.
     */
    for (ino=0; ino < nfiles; ino++) {
        /*
         * ROOTINO is the first i-node; skip any
         * before it.
         */
        if (ino < ROOTINO)
            continue;

        di = &dinode[ino];

        /*
         * If this is zero, the i-node is free (not
         * in use).
         */
        if ((di->di_mode & IFMT) == 0)
            continue;

        /*
         * Count the number of blocks being used by
         * this file.
         */
        if (di->di_uid >= 0 && di->di_uid < MAXUID)
            blocks[di->di_uid] += di->di_blocks;
    }

    /*
     * Print out what we added up.
     */
    printusage();
    exit(0);
}


/*
 * getsblock--get the super-block from the device
 *              referred to by fd.
 */
getsblock(fd)
int fd;
{
    /*
     * Make sure the disk information is current.
     * This causes all disk writes to be scheduled.
     */
    sync();

    /*
     * Read in the super-block.  It is stored at file
     * system block number SBLOCK.
     */
    bread(fd, SBLOCK, (char *) &sblock, SBSIZE);
```

```
     /*
      * The number of files (i-nodes) is calculated by
      * multiplying the number of i-nodes per cylinder
      * group by the number of cylinder groups.
      */
     nfiles = sblock.fs_ipg * sblock.fs_ncg;

     /*
      * Save the name of the file system.
      */
     filsys = sblock.fs_fsmnt;
}

/*
 * getinodes--read in the i-node structures from the device
 *            referred to by fd.
 */
getinodes(fd)
int fd;
{
     register ino_t ino;
     register daddr_t iblk;
     struct dinode *malloc();

     /*
      * Allocate space for them all.
      */
     dinode = malloc(nfiles * sizeof(struct dinode));

     if (dinode == NULL) {
         fprintf(stderr, "%s: out of memory.\n", pname);
         exit(1);
     }

     /*
      * We read in i-nodes a disk block-full at a time.
      * The INOPB macro returns the number of i-nodes
      * in a block; it uses the super-block to determine
      * the file system block size.
      */
     for (ino = 0; ino < nfiles; ino += INOPB(&sblock)) {
     /*
      * The i-node file system block number is given by
      * the itod macro.  The disk block number is computed
      * from the file system block number by the fsbtodb macro.
      */

        iblk = fsbtodb(&sblock, itod(&sblock, ino));

        /*
         * Read in this block of i-nodes.
         */
        bread(fd, iblk, (char *) &dinode[ino], sblock.fs_bsize);
```

```
        }
}

/*
 * bread-read cnt bytes form fd into buf, starting at
 *          address bno.
 */
bread(fd, bno, buf, cnt)
daddr_t bno;
char *buf;
int cnt;
{
    int n;

    /*
     * Seek to the proper block.  The dtob macro converts
     * the block number to a byte address.
     */
    lseek(fd, (long) dtob(bno), L_SET);

    /*
     * Round cnt up to a multiple of the device block size.
     */
    cnt = roundup(cnt, DEV_BSIZE);

    /*
     * Read in the data.
     */
    if ((n = read(fd, buf, cnt)) != cnt) {
        perror(filsys);
        exit(1);
    }
}

/*
 * printusage-print out the disk usage in blocks.
 */
printusage()
{
    register int i;
    struct passwd *pwd;

    printf("%s (%s):\n", device, filsys);
    printf(" Blocks \t   User\n");

    for (i=0; i < MAXUID; i++) {
        if (blocks[i] == 0)
            continue;

        /*
         * Look up the login name, and use it if we find it.
         */
        if ((pwd = getpwuid(i)) != NULL)
```

```
        printf("%8d\t%s\n", blocks[i], pwd->pw_name);
    else
        printf("%8d\t#%d\n", blocks[i], i);
    }
}
```

Generally, this program is almost identical to Example 13-1. The main differences involve the units used in some of the addresses, and the methods of converting between units. In the `getsblock` routine, the super-block is read using the `bread` function instead of doing it directly. This is because the location of the super-block is defined as a disk block number, not a byte address (granted, we could have converted it in the previous example). In the `getinodes` routine, the `itod` macro returns a file system block number, not a disk block number. This is then converted to a disk block number by the `fsbtodb` macro. Recall that file system blocks can be any multiple of 4096 bytes, while disk blocks are (usually) 512 bytes. Just below that point, note that the call to `bread` uses the `fs_bsize` element of the super-block structure instead of a defined constant block size. This is because, as mentioned previously, different file systems on the same machine can have different block sizes. Finally, note that in `bread`, the `dtob` macro is used to convert disk block numbers to byte offsets, instead of using a shift directly.

Reading Data Blocks From the File System

For most purposes, the information stored in the on-disk i-node structure is sufficient to complete whatever task is being performed. Occasionally, however, it is necessary to read the data blocks of the file(s) themselves. For example, the *dump* program on Berkeley systems reads the data blocks of each file on the disk in order to back the files up to tape.

The addresses of the data blocks associated with a file are stored in the `dinode` structure for that file. The first several addresses are direct addresses of blocks on the disk; they can be read by passing that address to the `bread` function of the previous examples. The next address is that of a singly indirect block. In order to use this block, it is first read in, and then treated as an array of direct block addresses. Similarly, the doubly indirect block is read in, and treated as an array of addresses of singly indirect blocks. Each of those singly indirect blocks is read in, and used as an array of direct block addresses. Finally, the triply indirect block is read in and treated as an array of addresses of doubly indirect blocks.

The above scenario readily translates into two small procedures, one to read the direct blocks of a file, and one to read all the indirect blocks. Example 13-3 shows these routines as they would be written for the Berkeley Fast File System; little modification is needed to make them run under System V.

Example 13-3. read_blocks—read data blocks from the raw disk

```
read_blocks(dp)
struct dinode *dp;
{
    int count;
    register int i, n;
    char dblock[MAXBSIZE];

    count = dp->di_size;

    /*
     * For each direct block in the file (NDADDR indicates
     * the number of direct addresses stored)...
     */
    for (i=0; (i < NDADDR) && (count > 0); i++) {
        /*
         * Read in the block from disk.  Read in count
         * bytes or a disk block, whichever is less.
         */
        bread(fsbtodb(&sblock, dp->di_db[i]), dblock,
                n = min(count, sblock.fs_bsize));
        count -= n;

        /* process data block ... */

    }

    /*
     * Now start reading the indirect blocks.  NIADDR is
     * the number of indirect addresses.  Recall that
     * the first indirect address is singly indirect,
     * the second is doubly indirect, an so on.
     */
    for (i=0; (i < NIADDR) && (count > 0); i++)
        read_indirect (dp->di_ib[i], i, &count);
}

/*
 * read_indirect--read the indirect blocks of the file.  The
 * level argument indicates our level of indirection; 0 is
 * singly indirect, 1 is doubly indirect, and so on.
 */
read_indirect (blkno, level, count)
ino_t blkno;
int *count;
int level;
{
```

```
register int i, n;
char dblock[MAXBSIZE];
daddr_t idblk[MAXBSIZE / sizeof(daddr_t)];

/*
 * Read in the block from disk.
 */
if (blkno)
    bread(fsbtodb(&sblock, blkno), idblk, sblock.fs_bsize);
else
    bzero(idblk, sblock.fs_bsize);

/*
 * If level is zero, then this block contains disk block
 * addresses, since blkno was a singly indirect address.
 * If level is non-zero, then this block contains addresses
 * of more indirect blocks.
 */
if (level <= 0) {
    /*
     * For each disk block (the NINDIR macro returns
     * the number of indirect addresses in a block)...
     */
    for (i=0; (i < NINDIR(&sblock)) && (*count > 0); i++) {
        /*
         * Read in the block from disk.
         */
        bread(fsbtodb(&sblock, idblk[i]), dblock,
                n = min(*count, sblock.fs_bsize));
        *count -= n;

        /* process data block ... */
    }

    /*
     * Done processing.
     */
    return;
}

/*
 * Decrement the level we're at.
 */
level--;

/*
 * Handle the next level of indirection by calling
 * ourselves recursively with each address in this
 * block.
 */
for (i=0; i < NINDIR(&sblock); i++)
    read_indirect(idblk[i], level, count);
}
```

The bread function is similar to that of Example 13-2, except that it requires a global file descriptor referring to the raw disk device, since that information is not passed to it by the calling routines.

Using the material described in this chapter, most functions requiring direct access to the disk can be performed. The only task which is not so simple is determining the name of a file given as its i-node number. To do this, the program must read all the directory data blocks stored on the disk, since the file's name is not stored with the file, but in the file's parent directory. To determine the complete path name of a file, this process must be repeated recursively until the root of the file system is reached. The code to do this is straightforward, but complex, and too long to present as an example here.

14

Miscellaneous Routines

Resource Limits
Obtaining Resource Usage Information
Manipulating Byte Strings
Environment Variables
The Current Working Directory
Searching for Characters in Strings
Determining Whether a File is a Terminal
Printing Error Messages
Sorting Arrays in Memory

This chapter describes some useful system calls and library routines whose descriptions don't fit well into the previous chapters. Many of the routines described here pertain only to Berkeley UNIX, as it provides many more functions than the other variants.

Resource Limits

Under Berkeley UNIX, each process operates with certain limits on the resources it may use. These limits prevent processes from creating files that are considered "too large," using too much CPU time, and so on.

The getrlimit System Call

The `getrlimit` system call is used by a process to obtain its current resource limits. It takes two arguments: a constant indicating the limit to be obtained, and a pointer to a structure of type `rlimit`, which will be filled in with the requested values. This structure is declared in the include file *sys/resource.h*; the files *sys/types.h* and *sys/time.h* must also be included:

```
struct rlimit {
    int     rlim_cur;       /* current (soft) limit        */
    int     rlim_max;       /* maximum value for rlim_cur */
};
```

The `rlim_cur` element of this structure indicates the current limit in effect for the process, `rlim_max` indicates the maximum value that `rlim_cur` may take on.

The constants which indicate which limit is to be selected are also defined in *sys/resource.h*. They are as follows:

RLIMIT_CPU	The maximum amount of CPU time, in milliseconds, that the process may use. If the process exceeds this limit, it will receive a SIGXCPU signal (see Chapter 8, *Processing Signals*).
RLIMIT_FSIZE	The maximum size, in bytes, of any file the process may create. If the process attempts to write a file larger than this size, it will receive a SIGXFSZ signal (see Chapter 8).
RLIMIT_DATA	The maximum size, in bytes, of the process's data segment. This includes memory allocated at program start-up as well as all dynamically allocated memory.
RLIMIT_STACK	The maximum size, in bytes, that the process's stack may grow to. If the process's stack exceeds this size, the process will receive a SIGILL signal (see Chapter 8).
RLIMIT_CORE	The largest size, in bytes, of a *core* file that may be created.
RLIMIT_RSS	The maximum size, in bytes, to which a process's *resident set size* may grow. This imposes a limit on the amount of physical memory that a process may use.

The setrlimit System Call

A process may change its limits by using the `setrlimit` system call. This call also takes two arguments: a constant indicating the limit to be changed, and a pointer to a structure of type `rlimit` containing the new values to be set. Any process may change its current limits; only the super-user may raise the maximum limits. `setrlimit` returns 0 if the call succeeds; –1 is returned if it does not and `errno` is set to the reason for failure.

The usual method for changing resource limits is shown in Example 14-1.

Example 14-1. setlim—change resource limits

```
#include <sys/types.h>
#include <sys/time.h>
#include <sys/resource.h>

/*
 * setlim--set the resource limit lim to the value val.
 */
setlim(lim, val)
int lim, val;
{
    struct rlimit rlim;

    /*
     * First get the current limits so we
     * will know the maximum value.
     */
    getrlimit(lim, &rlim);

    /*
     * Now change the current limit.
     */
    rlim.rlim_cur = val;

    /*
     * Now set the new limit.
     */
    return(setrlimit(lim, &rlim));
}
```

Obtaining Resource Usage Information

Berkeley UNIX maintains a great deal of information about the resources used by a process besides the amount of CPU time used. This information is obtained using the `getrusage` system call. This call takes two arguments: a constant indicating the information to be obtained, and a pointer to a structure or type `rusage`, which will contain the information on return. The constants, defined in the include file *sys/resource.h*, are:

RUSAGE_SELF   Obtain the resource usage information for the current process only.

RUSAGE_CHILDREN   Obtain the resource usage information for all terminated children of the current process.

The rusage structure, also declared in *sys/resource.h*, is shown below. The files *sys/types.h* and *sys/time.h* must also be included.

```
struct      rusage {
    struct timeval ru_utime;
    struct timeval ru_stime;
    long      ru_maxrss;
    long      ru_ixrss;
    long      ru_idrss;
    long      ru_isrss;
    long      ru_minflt;
    long      ru_majflt;
    long      ru_nswap;
    long      ru_inblock;
    long      ru_oublock;
    long      ru_msgsnd;
    long      ru_msgrcv;
    long      ru_nsignals;
    long      ru_nvcsw;
    long      ru_nivcsw;
};
```

The fields are interpreted as follows:

ru_utime   The total amount of time spent executing in user mode.

ru_stime   The total amount of time spent in the system executing on behalf of the process(es).

ru_maxrss   The maximum resident set size utilized (in kilobytes).

ru_ixrss   An "integral" value indicating the amount of memory used by the text segment that was also shared among other processes. This value is expressed in units of *kilobytes × seconds-of-execution* and is calculated by summing the number of shared memory pages in use each time the internal system clock ticks and then averaging over one second intervals.

ru_idrss   An integral value of the amount of unshared memory residing in the data segment. Expressed in units of *kilobytes × seconds-of-execution* .

ru_isrss   An integral value of the amount of unshared memory residing in the stack segment. Expressed in units of *kilobytes × seconds-of-execution* .

ru_minflt   The number of page faults serviced without any I/O activity; this is done by "reclaiming" a page frame from the list of pages awaiting reallocation.

ru_majflt   The number of page faults serviced that required I/O activity.

ru_nswap   The number of times the process was "swapped" out of main memory.

ru_inblock   The number of times the file system had to perform input.

ru_oublock   The number of times the file system had to perform output.

ru_msgsnd   The number of I/O messages sent.

ru_msgrcv   The number of I/O messages received.

ru_nsignals The number of signals delivered to the process.

ru_nvcsw   The number of times a context switch resulted due to a process voluntarily giving up the processor before its time slice was completed. (This is usually done to await the availability of a resource.)

ru_nivcsw   The number of times a context switch resulted due to a higher priority process becoming runnable or because the current process exceeded its time slice.

Manipulating Byte Strings

System V and Berkeley UNIX both provide several library routines for manipulating arbitrary strings of bytes. Most programmers should be aware of the "standard" string manipulation routines: strcmp, strcpy, strncmp, and strncpy. Although these routines work fine for strings of printable characters, they do not work well when they must cross over null bytes and so on. Here we'll discuss various routines that can be useful for handling special cases.

The bcmp and memcmp Library Routines

In Berkeley UNIX, the bcmp routine may be used to compare two arbitrary byte strings. It takes three arguments: two character pointers to the strings to be compared, and an integer number of bytes to be compared. It returns 0 if the two strings are equal, non-zero otherwise.

In System V, this function is performed by the memcmp routine, which also takes three arguments, in the same order. Unlike bcmp, memcmp acts exactly like strcmp, and returns a value less than, greater than, or equal to 0 indicating that the string pointed to by the first argument is lexicographically less than, greater than, or identical to the string pointed to by the second argument.

The bcopy and memcpy Library Routines

In Berkeley UNIX, the bcopy library routine may be used to copy arbitrary byte strings. It takes three arguments: a character pointer to the source string, a character pointer to the destination string, and an integer number of bytes to copy. The routine *always* copies the requested number of bytes; it does not stop at a null byte as strncpy does.

In System V, the memcpy routine performs the same function. This routine also takes three arguments: a character pointer to the destination string, a character pointer to the source string, and an integer number of bytes to copy. Note that memcpy uses the same argument order for the source and destination strings that strncpy does, while bcopy reverses the order.

The bzero and memset Library Routines

In Berkeley UNIX, the bzero routine may be used to set an arbitrary number of bytes to zero. It takes two arguments: a pointer to the memory to be zeroed, and an integer number of bytes to zero. This routine is useful for zeroing large character arrays, structures, and so on.

System V provides a more generic routine, memset. This routine takes three arguments: a character pointer to the memory to be set, a character to set each byte of the memory to, and an integer number of bytes to set. To make memset emulate bzero, the call:

```
memset (s, '\0', n)
```

would be used.

Environment Variables

As mentioned in Chapter 9, *Executing Programs*, each program has an *environment* when it is executing. The environment contains several variables of the form NAME=*value*. This is where information such as the program's search path, the user's login name, the terminal type, and so on are stored.

To obtain the value of one of these variables, the getenv routine is used. This routine takes one argument, a character string containing the name of the variable to be returned (e.g., "TERM"). It returns a pointer to the value of that variable (a character string) if the variable exists, or the constant NULL if it does not.

The Current Working Directory

Berkeley UNIX provides a library routine that a program may use to obtain the path name of its current working directory. This routine, getwd, takes a single argument, a pointer to a character string in which to store the name of the directory. In 4.1BSD, this routine was stored in the *-ljobs* library; it has since been moved into the standard C library. The size of the string should be MAXPATHLEN characters; this constant is defined in the include file *sys/param.h*.

System V provides a similar routine, getcwd. This routine takes two arguments, a pointer to a character string in which to store the name of the directory, and an integer indicating the length of this string.

Searching for Characters in Strings

All versions of UNIX provide library routines to search for a character in a string. In Version 7 and the Berkeley distributions this routine is called index; it has been renamed strchr in System V. Both routines take two arguments, a pointer to a character string to be searched, and the character to search for. They return a character pointer pointing to the first occurrence of the character in the string on success, or the constant NULL on failure.

index and strchr search the string from the beginning until the first occurrence of the character is found. To search the string from the end toward the beginning, in order to locate the last occurrence of the character, the routines rindex (Berkeley UNIX) and strrchr (System V) should be used instead.

Determining Whether a File is a Terminal

Sometimes it is necessary for a program to know whether it is writing to a terminal or to a file. For example, the Berkeley UNIX *more* program does not prompt the user a page at a time unless it is sending output to a terminal.

The isatty Library Routine

The `isatty` library routine takes a single argument, an integer file descriptor. It returns non-zero if the file descriptor refers to a terminal device, and 0 otherwise. Thus, the *more* program uses a code segment such as the one shown below to determine whether or not to prompt the user a page at a time:

```
if (isatty(1))      /* check standard output */
    printprompt = YES;
else
    printprompt = NO;
```

The ttyname Library Routine

Programs also sometimes need to know the pathname of the terminal they are outputting to. This can be obtained using the `ttyname` library routine. It takes a single argument, an integer file descriptor, and returns a pointer to a character string containing the pathname to the terminal device that file descriptor refers to. If the file descriptor does not refer to a terminal device, the constant NULL is returned.

The /dev/tty Device

If a program needs to open its controlling terminal, but does not know the name of the terminal it is running on, it may open the pseudo-device */dev/tty*. For each process on the system, opening this device will actually open that process's controlling terminal.

Printing Error Messages

The perror Library Routine

Throughout this book, the `perror` library routine has been used to print error messages when errors occur. As mentioned previously, whenever a system call (but not a library routine) fails, it returns –1 and sets the external integer `errno` to a value indicating the specific error which occurred.

Character strings describing each of these errors are stored in the external array of character pointers called `sys_errlist`. Additionally, constants allowing the program to check for specific errors are defined in the include file *errno.h*.

The `perror` library routine takes a single argument, a character string. It prints this string, followed by a colon, followed by the character string from `sys_errlist` that describes the error number contained in `errno` on the standard error output.

The psignal Library Routine

Berkeley UNIX provides another routine similar to `perror` called `psignal`. This routine accepts two arguments: an integer signal number, and a pointer to a character string. It prints the character string, followed by a colon, followed by a character string describing the signal on the standard error output. The character strings describing the signals are contained in the external array of character pointers called `sys_siglist`.

Sorting Arrays in Memory

Often it is necessary to sort the elements of an array in memory. This is easily done using the `qsort` library routine, which uses the quicksort algorithm to sort arbitrary data structures in memory. It takes four arguments: a pointer to the start of the array, an integer indicating the number of elements in the array, an integer indicating the size of each element in bytes, and a pointer to a comparison routine. The comparison routine should accept two arguments, pointers to two array elements to be compared. It should return an integer less than, greater than, or equal to zero depending on whether the first element is considered less than, greater than, or equal to the second element.

Example 14-2 shows a program that reads ten strings from the standard input into an array and prints them out sorted in ascending and then descending order.

Example 14-2. qsort—demonstrate `qsort` *routine*

```
#include <stdio.h>

#define NSTRS    10        /* number of strings     */
#define STRLEN   16        /* length of each string */

char strs[NSTRS][STRLEN];  /* array of strings      */

main()
{
    int i;
    extern int compare1(), compare2();
```

```
        /*
         * Prompt the user for NSTRS strings.
         */
        for (i=0; i < NSTRS; i++) {
            printf("Enter string #%d: ", i);
            (void) fgets(strs[i], sizeof(strs[0]), stdin);
        }

        /*
         * Sort the strings into ascending order.  There
         * are NSTRS array elements, each one is STRLEN
         * characters long.  Note we give the size of
         * the array element, not the length of the
         * string in it.
         */
        qsort(strs, NSTRS, STRLEN, compare1);

        /*
         * Print the strings.
         */
        printf("\nSorted in ascending order:\n");

        for (i=0; i < NSTRS; i++)
            printf("\t%s", strs[i]);

        /*
         * Now sort the strings in descending order.
         */
        qsort(strs, NSTRS, STRLEN, compare2);

        printf("\nSorted in descending order:\n");

        for (i=0; i < NSTRS; i++)
            printf("\t%s", strs[i]);

        exit(0);
    }

    /*
     * compare1--compare a and b, and return less than,
     *           greater than, or equal to zero.  Since
     *           we are comparing character strings, we
     *           can just use strcmp to do the work for us.
     */
    compare1(a, b)
    char *a, *b;
    {
        return(strcmp(a, b));
    }

    /*
     * compare2--this compares a and b, but is used for
     *           sorting in the opposite order.  Thus it
```

```
 *              returns the opposite of strcmp.  We can
 *              simulate this by simply reversing the
 *              arguments when we call strcmp.
 */
compare2(a, b)
char *a, *b;
{
    return(strcmp(b, a));
}
```

A

Calling FORTRAN From C

Data Representation
Procedure Naming
Returning Values from Functions
Passing Arguments
Input and Output
Libraries
Further Information

The UNIX C and FORTRAN compilers were written to use the same object code format. This feature permits the programmer to call FORTRAN functions from C programs, and vice-versa. FORTRAN programs can thus use many of the C library functions and system calls, and C programs can call functions from FORTRAN libraries.

Note that the information in this appendix is based on the Berkeley UNIX C and FORTRAN compilers on DEC VAX hardware. There may be some differences in variable sizes and compiler specifics on other hardware or other versions of the operating system.

Data Representation

The following is a table of corresponding FORTRAN and C variable declarations:

FORTRAN	C
`integer*2 x`	`short x;`
`integer x`	`long x;`
`logical x`	`long x;`
`real x`	`float x;`
`double precision x`	`double x;`
`complex x`	`struct { float real, imag; } x;`
`double complex x`	`struct { double real, imag; } x;`
`character*10 x`	`char x[10];`

(By the rules of FORTRAN, `integer`, `logical`, and `real` occupy the same amount of memory.)

It should be noted that when dealing with arrays, C arrays are indexed from 0 to N–1, while FORTRAN arrays are indexed from 1 to N by default. FORTRAN arrays may be made to index from 0 by declaring them as `array(0:N-1)` instead of `array(N)`.

One last thing about arrays—C stores arrays in row-major order, while FORTRAN stores them in column-major order. This means that if a two-dimensional array in C is subscripted as `array[i][j]`, the same array in FORTRAN would be subscripted as `array(j,i)`. Likewise, the dimensions of the array would be reversed when declaring it in the two languages.

Procedure Naming

The FORTRAN compiler appends an underscore character ('_') to each user-defined common block or procedure. The purpose is to avoid conflicts with C procedures and variables of the same name (most of the FORTRAN libraries are written in C). Unfortunately, it means the programmer must be careful when naming his or her procedures.

Naming C Routines to be Called From FORTRAN

In order for a procedure written in C to be callable from a FORTRAN program, its name must end with an underscore. The underscore is not used in the FORTRAN program by the programmer, rather it is appended automatically by the compiler. Recall that FORTRAN procedure names may be no longer than six characters; the underscore is not counted. For example:

FORTRAN Routine	C Routine

```
integer i              hello_()   /* note underscore */
                       {
i = 5                       printf("Hello, world.\n");
call hello             }

stop
end
```

Naming FORTRAN Routines to be Called From C

When calling FORTRAN from C, the C program must supply the underscore on the procedure name. The FORTRAN compiler will add it automatically in the FORTRAN program. For example:

C Routine	FORTRAN Routine

```
main()                 subroutine hello
{
    hello_();          print *, 'Hello, world.'
}                      end
```

Returning Values from Functions

Integer, Logical, Real, Double Precision

Functions that return `integer`, `logical`, `real`, and `double` precision values are simply declared as such and just return their values as defined in the language. For example:

C Routine	FORTRAN Routine
| ```
main()
{
    long i;
    extern long y_();

    i = y_();
}

long x_()
{
    return(5L);
}
``` | ```
integer j
integer x

j = x()

stop
end

integer function y()

y = 10
end
``` |

Complex and Double Complex

A FORTRAN function that returns `complex` or `double complex` is equivalent to a C routine with an initial argument that points to the place where the return value is to be stored. For example:

C Routine	FORTRAN Routine
| ```
typedef struct { float r, i }
complex;

main()
{
    extern complex y_();
    complex i;

    y_(&i);
}

x_(c)
complex *c;
{
    c->r = 1.0;
    c->i = 2.0;
}
``` | ```
complex j
complex x

j = x()

stop
end

complex function y()

y = (1.0, 2.0)

end
``` |

Character Strings

A character-valued FORTRAN function is equivalent to a C routine with two initial arguments: a pointer and a length. For example:

C Routine	FORTRAN Routine

```
main ()                          character*15 j
{                                character*15 x
    extern char *y_();
    char i[15];                  j = x()

    y_(i, 15L);                  stop
}                                end

x_(s, len)
char *s;                         character*15 function y()
long len;
{                                y = 'abcdefghijklmno'
    s[0] = 'a';
    s[1] = 'b';                  end
    ...
    s[14] = 'o';
}
```

Passing Arguments

Unlike C, which allows arguments to procedures to be call-by-value or call-by-reference, FORTRAN requires all arguments to be call-by-reference. This tends to make calling FORTRAN from C somewhat inconvenient, since passing a single constant (e.g., 3) requires declaring a temporary variable, assigning it the value, and passing its address to the function.

The programmer must also be careful assigning values to procedure parameters—because they are all passed by address, assignments made inside functions and subroutines affect the variables in the main program.

Integers, Floats (Reals), and Doubles

These variables are simply passed by address; nothing else need be done. For example:

C Routine	FORTRAN Routine
| ```
main()
{
    long a, b, c;

    a = 4;
    b = 5;
    c = 6;

    y_(&a, &b, &c);
}

x_(u, v, w)
long *u, *v, *w;
{
    *u *= 2;
    *v *= 3;
    *w *= 4;
}
``` | ```
integer i, j, k

i = 1
j = 2
k = 3

call x(i, j, k)

stop
end

subroutine y(u, v, w)
integer u, v, w
u = u * 2
v = v * 3
w = w * 4

end
``` |

Following the execution of these programs, a will be 8, b will be 15, c will be 24, i will be 2, j will be 6, and k will be 12.

Characters and Logicals

Single characters and `logical` variables are also simply passed by address. The values 0 and 1 correspond to .FALSE. and .TRUE., respectively.

Character Strings

Character strings are also passed by address. However, an additional parameter follows all the declared parameters. This is a value parameter indicating the size of the character string. For example:

C Routine	FORTRAN Routine
| ```
main()
{
    char *i;

    i = "hi there";

    y_(s, 8L);
}

x_(s, len)
char *s;
long len;
{
    write(1, s, len);
}
``` | ```
character*15 j

j = 'abcdefghijklmno'

call x(j)

stop
end

subroutine y(s)
character*15 s

write(6,*) s

end
``` |

Functions

Passing procedures to and from routines is also possible; simply pass the address of the procedure as if it were a character string, and indicate its length as zero.

Overall Argument Sequence

The overall order of arguments passed to procedures is as follows:

1. Extra arguments for complex and character functions.
2. Pointer to each datum or function.
3. An integer value parameter for each character string or procedure.

For example, the call in:

```
external f
character*7 s
integer b(3)

call sam(f, b(2), s)
```

is equivalent to that in:

```
int f();
char s[7];
long b[3];

sam_(f, &b[1], s, 0, 7);
```

Input and Output

Input and output from most programs is normally done using the standard input (the keyboard), standard output (the screen), and the standard error output (also the screen). In C programs, these "devices" correspond to file descriptors 0, 1, and 2, respectively. In FORTRAN, they correspond to units 5, 6, and 0.

From C Programs

C programs calling FORTRAN routines that may do input or output should call the function f_init before anything else. This sets up the FORTRAN I/O library. If this routine is not called, any reads done by the FORTRAN routines will fail, and any output will be written to the file *fort.unit*, where *unit* is the unit number that was written to.

Before exiting, a call should be made to f_exit, to flush buffers, close files, etc.

From FORTRAN Programs

Doing output from C routines called by FORTRAN programs is generally not recommended. It requires the programmer to rearrange his or her file descriptors such that standard input is now 5, and so on. If you must do this, see the manual page on the dup system call.

Libraries

Several libraries must be loaded when compiling programs that mix languages. In general, FORTRAN programs that call C routines should be compiled as:

```
f77 file.f FORTRAN-libraries... -lc
```

and C programs that call FORTRAN routines should be compiled as:

```
cc file.c C-libraries... -lU77 -lF77 -lI77 -lm
```

Further Information

A much more detailed description of the internals of the FORTRAN and C language systems can be found in the documents shown below.

Feldman, S. J., Weinberger, P. J., and Berkman, J., *A Portable Fortran 77 Compiler*, UNIX Programmer's Supplementary Documents, Volume 1, 4.3 Berkeley Software Distribution, Virtual VAX-11 Version, April, 1986.

Wasley, David L. and Berkman, J., *An Introduction to the f77 I/O Library*, UNIX Programmer's Supplementary Documents, Volume 1, 4.3 Berkeley Software Distribution, Virtual VAX-11 Version, April, 1986.

Johnson, S. C., *A Tour Through the Portable C Compiler*, UNIX System Manager's Manual, 4.3 Berkeley Software Distribution, Virtual VAX-11 Version, April, 1986.

B

Using Berkeley Pseudo Terminals

Occasionally it is useful to be able to execute a program on a terminal, but to have the input and output of that terminal be connected to a program, rather than to a keyboard and screen. This is how the Berkeley UNIX *script* program works. *script* runs a program (usually a shell) on a terminal, and copies all the input and output to that terminal to a file called *typescript*.

The way this is done is by using devices called *pseudo terminals*. A pseudo terminal is actually made up of two devices, a *master* and a *slave*. The slave device has a name something like */dev/ttyp0* , while the master has a name such as */dev/ptyp0* . The last two characters of the name usually range from 'p' through 's' for the first character, and '0' through '9' and 'a' through 'f' for the second, providing a total of 64 pseudo terminals.

To use a pseudo terminal, the process opens the master side of the device for reading and writing. It then forks and executes the process to be controlled after making the child process's controlling terminal the slave side of the device.* Now,

---

*Executing programs is discussed in Chapter 9, *Executing Programs*; the controlling terminal is described in Chapter 10, *Job Control*.

when the process writes to the master side of the pseudo terminal, the program will receive the data as if it were typed on a terminal keyboard. When the program prints to its standard output or standard error output as if it were writing to a terminal screen, the process may read this output by reading from the master side of the pseudo terminal.

The program shown below implements a subroutine that takes three arguments: a character string containing a command to be executed, a pointer to a file pointer of type FILE to be used for sending input to the command, and a pointer to a file pointer of type FILE to be used for reading output from the command. The routine obtains a pseudo terminal and sets it up to be used by the command, and then executes the command and sets up the file pointers to be used. The routine returns 0 if this all succeeds, –1 if it fails.

Example B-1. ptyopen—open a pseudo-tty and execute a process on it

```
#include <sys/param.h>
#include <sys/ioctl.h>
#include <sys/file.h>
#include <signal.h>
#include <stdio.h>

ptyopen(cmd, ifp, ofp)
char *cmd;
FILE **ifp, **ofp;
{
    int i;
    char *args[16];
    register int tty;
    long ldisc, lmode;
    register char *s, *t;
    struct sgttyb sgttyb;
    struct tchars tchars;
    struct ltchars ltchars;
    char ttybuf[16], ptybuf[16];

    /*
     * Split up the arguments in the command
     * into an argv-like structure.
     */
    i = 0;
    s = cmd;

    while (*s) {
        /*
         * Skip white space.
         */
        while ((*s == ' ') || (*s == '\t'))
            *s++ = '\0';
```

```
            args[i++] = s;

            /*
             * Skip over this word to next white space.
             */
            while ((*s != '\0') && (*s != ' ') && (*s != '\t'))
                s++;
    }

    args[i] = NULL;

    /*
     * Get a pseudo-tty.  We do this by cycling through all
     * the possible names.  The operating system will not
     * allow us to open a master which is already in use,
     * so we simply go until the open succeeds.
     */
    for (s = "pqrs"; *s != '\0'; s++) {
        for (t = "0123456789abcdef"; *t != '\0'; t++) {
            sprintf(ptybuf, "/dev/pty%c%c", *s, *t);

            if ((tty = open(ptybuf, O_RDWR)) >= 0)
                goto out;
        }
    }

out:
    /*
     * If s and t are NULL, we ran out of pseudo ttys
     * before we found one we can use.
     */
    if ((*s == '\0') && (*t == '\0'))
        return(-1);

    /*
     * Change "ptyXX" (master) to "ttyXX" (slave).
     */
    strcpy(ttybuf, ptybuf);
    ttybuf[5] = 't';

    /*
     * Get the modes of the current terminal.  We
     * will duplicate these on the pseudo terminal.
     */
    ioctl(0, TIOCGETD, &ldisc);
    ioctl(0, TIOCLGET, &lmode);
    ioctl(0, TIOCGETP, &sgttyb);
    ioctl(0, TIOCGETC, &tchars);
    ioctl(0, TIOCGLTC, &ltchars);

    /*
     * Fork a child process.
     */
```

```
if ((i = fork()) < 0) {
    close(tty);
    return(-1);
}

/*
 * In the child...
 */
if (i == 0) {
    /*
     * Close all open files.
     */
    for (i=0; i < NOFILE; i++)
        close(i);

    /*
     * Clear the controlling tty.  This means
     * that we will not have a controlling
     * tty until we open another terminal
     * device.
     */
    if ((i = open("/dev/tty", O_RDWR)) >= 0) {
        ioctl(i, TIOCNOTTY, 0);
        close(i);
    }

    /*
     * Make our controlling tty the pseudo tty.
     * This happens because we cleared our
     * original controlling terminal above.
     */
    i = open(ttybuf, O_RDWR);

    /*
     * Set stdin, stdout, and stderr to be the
     * pseudo terminal.
     */
    dup2(i, 0);
    dup2(i, 1);
    dup2(i, 2);

    /*
     * Set the pseudo terminal's tty modes to
     * those of the original terminal.  We
     * turn off ECHO and CBREAK modes, since
     * we don't want characters "typed" to be
     * printed.
     */
    sgttyb.sg_flags &= ~ECHO;
    sgttyb.sg_flags &= ~CRMOD;

    ioctl(0, TIOCSETD, &ldisc);
    ioctl(0, TIOCLGET, &lmode);
```

```
        ioctl(0, TIOCSETP, &sgttyb);
        ioctl(0, TIOCSETC, &tchars);
        ioctl(0, TIOCSLTC, &ltchars);

        /*
         * Set the process group of the process
         * to be the process group of the
         * terminal.
         */
        ioctl(0, TIOCGPGRP, &i);
        setpgrp(0, i);

        /*
         * Now change the process group of the
         * terminal and process to be the
         * process id; this takes them out
         * of the calling process's process
         * group.
         */
        i = getpid();

        ioctl(0, TIOCSPGRP, &i);
        setpgrp(0, i);

        /*
         * Execute the program.
         */
        execv(*args, args);

        exit(1);
    }

    /*
     * Set up the input and output file pointers
     * so that they can write and read the pseudo
     * terminal.
     */
    *ifp = fdopen(tty, "w");
    *ofp = fdopen(tty, "r");

    return(0);
}
```

C

Reading Kernel Data Structures

NOTE

The discussion in this section applies to Berkeley UNIX. Although the principles are the same for System V and Version 7 UNIX, there are some slight differences that are not discussed here.

Many system programs, such as *ps*, *uptime*, *w*, and so on print out information by reading data directly from operating system memory. This is done by reading the device */dev/kmem*, which is essentially a window into the memory being used by the operating system, called "kernel memory." Reading from this device actually copies data from operating system memory into the user's program. Because much of the information in operating system memory should be kept private for security reasons, opening the file */dev/kmem* is often restricted to the super-user.

In order to obtain interesting information by reading */dev/kmem*, a process must know the addresses of the data structures it wishes to access. To do this, the nlist library routine is used. This routine takes two arguments: a character string naming an executable file (*a.out*), and a pointer to an array of structures of type nlist. This structure is declared in the include file *nlist.h*; *sys/types.h* must also be included:

```
struct nlist {
    char    *n_name;        /* for use when in-core   */
    unsigned char n_type;   /* type flag, i.e. N_TEXT */
    char    n_other;        /* unused                 */
    short   n_desc;         /* see <stab.h>           */
    unsigned long n_value;  /* value of this symbol   */
};
```

Before calling `nlist`, the calling program should set the n_name elements of these structures to the names of the variables it wants to find. After calling `nlist`, the n_value elements will contain the addresses in the named file where these variables are stored.

`nlist` operates by reading the *symbol table* in an executable file, which is created by the compiler. Normally, the information obtained this way is used by debuggers and the like to modify variable values, etc. However, for reading kernel data structures, the use is slightly different. Rather than using the addresses obtained to access the executable program that is the operating system (*/vmunix*), they are used to access the memory being used by the operating system by reading */dev/kmem* .

The program below accesses */dev/kmem* to read the variables _boottime and _avenrun. The first of these variables is the time the system was last started ("booted"). The second indicates the *load average* , an average over time of the number of runnable processes in the system. Note the types of the variables—there is unfortunately no standard documentation that describes kernel data structures and which ones are of what type; this is something that can only be learned by examining the operating system source code.

Example C-1. kmem—demonstrate how to read kernel memory

```
#include <sys/param.h>
#include <sys/time.h>
#include <sys/file.h>
#include <nlist.h>
#include <stdio.h>

/*
 * We declare an array of nlist structures,
 * and initialize them to the names of the
 * variables we want.  The last entry is
 * to terminate the list.
 */
```

```
        struct nlist nl[] = {
#define X_BOOTTIME      0
        {     "_boottime" },
#define X_AVENRUN       1
        {     "_avenrun" },
        {     0          }
};

main()
{
    int kmem;
    char *ctime();
    struct timeval boottime;

    /*
     * _avenrun is an array of three numbers.
     * Most machines use floating point; Sun
     * workstations use long integers.
     */
#ifdef sun
    long avenrun[3];
#else
    double avenrun[3];
#endif

    /*
     * Open kernel memory.
     */
    if ((kmem = open("/dev/kmem", O_RDONLY)) < 0) {
        perror("/dev/kmem");
        exit(1);
    }

    /*
     * Read the kernel namelist.  If nl[0].n_type is
     * 0 after this, then the call to nlist() failed.
     */
    if ((nlist("/vmunix", nl) < 0) || (nl[0].n_type == 0)) {
        fprintf(stderr, "/vmunix: no namelist\n");
        exit(1);
    }

    /*
     * Read the _boottime variable.  We do this by
     * seeking through memory to the address found
     * by nlist, and then reading.
     */
    lseek(kmem, (long) nl[X_BOOTTIME].n_value, L_SET);
    read(kmem, (char *) &boottime, sizeof(boottime));
```

```
    /*
     * Read the load averages.
     */
    lseek(kmem, (long) nl[X_AVENRUN].n_value, L_SET);
    read(kmem, (char *) avenrun, sizeof(avenrun));

    /*
     * Now print the system boot time.
     */
    printf("System booted at %s\n", ctime(&boottime.tv_sec));

    /*
     * Print the load averages.  Sun workstations use
     * FSCALE to convert the long integers to floating
     * point.  The three elements of _avenrun are the
     * load average over the past one, five, and ten
     * minutes.
     */
#ifdef sun
    printf("One minute load average:  %.2f\n",
        (double) avenrun[0] / FSCALE);
    printf("Five minute load average: %.2f\n",
        (double) avenrun[1] / FSCALE);
    printf("Ten minute load average:  %.2f\n",
        (double) avenrun[2] / FSCALE);
#else
    printf("One minute load average:  %.2f\n", avenrun[0]);
    printf("Five minute load average: %.2f\n", avenrun[1]);
    printf("Ten minute load average:  %.2f\n", avenrun[2]);
#endif

    close(kmem);
    exit(0);
}
```

D

Berkeley UNIX Directory Compatibility Routines

The code below is a public-domain implementation of the Berkeley UNIX directory routines described in Chapter 4, *Files and Directories*, These routines are intended for use on non-Berkeley UNIX systems, in order to allow the writing of portable code. Users of Berkeley UNIX systems will not need these routines, since equivalent ones are provided as part of the operating system.

```
#include <sys/types.h>
#include <sys/stat.h>
#include <sys/dir.h>
#include <stdio.h>

#define DIRSIZE(e)      (min(strlen(e->d_name), DIRSIZ))

typedef struct {
    int     d_fd;
} DIR;

char *malloc();

DIR *
opendir(dir)
char *dir;
```

```
{
    struct stat stbuf;
    DIR *dp = (DIR *) malloc(sizeof *dp);

    if ((dp->d_fd = open(dir, 0)) < 0)
        return(0);

    if ((fstat(dp->d_fd, &stbuf) < 0) ||
        ((stbuf.st_mode & S_IFDIR) == 0)) {
        closedir(dp);
        return(0);      /* this isn't a directory! */
    }
    return(dp);
}

closedir(dp)
DIR *dp;
{
    (void) close(dp->d_fd);
    free((char *) dp);
}

struct direct *
readdir(dp)
DIR *dp;
{
    static struct direct dir;

    do {
        if (read(dp->d_fd, &dir, sizeof(dir)) != sizeof(dir))
            return(0);
    } while (dir.d_ino == 0);

    return(&dir);
}

/*
 * Scandir returns the number of entries or -1 if the
 * directory cannot be opened or malloc fails.
 */
scandir(dir, nmptr, select, compar)
char *dir;
char ***nmptr;
int (*select)();
int (*compar)();
{
    DIR *dirp;
    char **array;
    char **realloc();
    struct direct *ent;
    unsigned int nalloc = 10, nentries = 0;

    if ((dirp = opendir(dir)) == NULL)
```

```
                return(-1);

        array = (char **) malloc(nalloc * sizeof (char *));

        if (array == NULL)
                return(-1);

        while ((ent = readdir(dirp)) != NULL) {
                if (select && ((*select)(ent->d_name) == 0))
                        continue;

                if (nentries == nalloc) {
                        array = realloc(array, (nalloc += 10) * sizeof(char *));

                        if (array == NULL)
                                return(-1);
                }

                array[nentries] = (char *) malloc(DIRSIZE(ent)+1);
                strncpy(array[nentries], ent->d_name, DIRSIZE(ent));
                array[nentries][DIRSIZE(ent)] = NULL;
                nentries++;
        }

        closedir(dirp);

        if ((nentries + 1) != nalloc)
                array = realloc(array, ((nentries + 1) * sizeof (char *)));

        if (compar != 0)
                qsort(array, nentries, sizeof(char **), compar);

        *nmptr = array;
        array[nentries] = 0;        /* guaranteed 0 pointer */

        return(nentries);
}

alphasort(a, b)
char **a, **b;
{
        return(strcmp(*a, *b));
}
```

Interval Timer
Version of nap()

The code below is an interval timer version (see Chapter 7, *Telling Time and Timing Things*) of the nap routine. This routine is much like sleep, except that it works in units of sixtieths of a second, instead of in units of seconds. This code will work only on Berkeley UNIX systems.

```
#include <sys/time.h>
#include <signal.h>

#define setvec(vec, a) \
            vec.sv_handler = a; \
            vec.sv_mask = vec.sv_flags = 0

static int ringring;

nap(n)
unsigned n;
{
    void napx();
    long omask;
    struct sigvec vec, ovec;
    struct itimerval itv, oitv;
    register struct itimerval *itp = &itv;
```

```
        if (n == 0)
            return;

        timerclear(&itp->it_interval);
        timerclear(&itp->it_value);

        if (setitimer(ITIMER_REAL, itp, &oitv) < 0)
            return;

        setvec(ovec, SIG_DFL);
        omask = sigblock(sigmask(SIGALRM));

        itp->it_value.tv_sec = n/60;
        itp->it_value.tv_usec = (n%60)*1000000/60;

        if (timerisset(&oitv.it_value)) {
            if (oitv.it_value.tv_sec >= itp->it_value.tv_sec) {
                if (oitv.it_value.tv_sec == itp->it_value.tv_sec &&
                    oitv.it_value.tv_usec > itp->it_value.tv_usec)
                    oitv.it_value.tv_usec -= itp->it_value.tv_usec;
                        oitv.it_value.tv_sec -= itp->it_value.tv_sec;
            }
            else {
                itp->it_value = oitv.it_value;

                /*
                 * This is a hack, but we must have time to return from
                 * the setitimer after the alarm or else it will restart.
                 * And, anyway, sleep never did more than this before.
                 */
                oitv.it_value.tv_sec = 1;
                oitv.it_value.tv_usec = 0;
            }
        }

        setvec(vec, napx);
        ringring = 0;

        sigvec(SIGALRM, &vec, &ovec);
        setitimer(ITIMER_REAL, itp, (struct itimerval *)0);

        while (!ringring)
            sigpause(omask &~ sigmask(SIGALRM));

        sigvec(SIGALRM, &ovec, (struct sigvec *)0);
        setitimer(ITIMER_REAL, &oitv, (struct itimerval *)0);
        sigsetmask(omask);
}

static void
napx()
{
        ringring = 1;
}
```

Bibliography

This bibliography lists a few books and several papers in the *UNIX Programmer's Manual* which discuss many aspects of UNIX programming. Although the references here are to the 4.3BSD version of the *UNIX Programmer's Manual* (UPM), many of the documents are also contained in other versions as well.

The System V Interface Definition , American Telephone and Telegraph Company, 1986.

UNIX System V Release 2.0 Interprocess Communication Utilities Guide , American Telephone and Telegraph Company, October, 1984.

Joy, William, Fabry, Robert, Leffler, Samuel, McKusick, M. Kirk, and Karels, Michael, *Berkeley Software Architecture Manual, 4.3BSD Edition* , UNIX Programmer's Manual, 4.3BSD, Programmer's Supplementary Documents Volume 1, April, 1986.

Kernighan, Brian W. and Pike, Rob, *The UNIX Programming Environment* , Prentice-Hall, 1984.

Kernighan, Brian W. and Ritchie, Dennis M., *The C Programming Language*, Prentice-Hall, 1978.

Kernighan, Brian W. and Ritchie, Dennis M., *UNIX Programming—Second Edition*, UNIX Programmer's Manual, 4.3BSD, Programmer's Supplementary Documents Volume 2, April, 1986. Originally published in the Version 7 UPM, 1977.

Leffler, Samuel J., Fabry, Robert S., Joy, William N., Lapsley, Phil, Miller, Steve, and Torek, Chris, *An Advanced 4.3BSD Interprocess Communication Tutorial*, UNIX Programmer's Manual, 4.3BSD, Programmer's Supplementary Documents Volume 1, April, 1986.

Ritchie, Dennis M., *The UNIX I/O System*, UNIX Programmer's Manual, 4.3BSD, Programmer's Supplementary Documents Volume 2, April, 1986. Originally published in the Version 7 UPM, 1977.

Ritchie, D. M. and Thompson, K., *The UNIX Time-Sharing System*, UNIX Programmer's Manual, 4.3BSD, Programmer's Supplementary Documents Volume 2, April, 1986. Originally published in the Version 6 UPM, 1975.

Sechrest, Stuart, *An Introductory 4.3BSD Interprocess Communication Tutorial*, UNIX Programmer's Manual, 4.3BSD, Programmer's Supplementary Documents Volume 1, April, 1986.

Technical Committee on Operating Systems of the IEEE Computer Society, *IEEE Trial Use Standard: Portable Operating System for Computer Environments*, IEEE, 1986.

Thompson, K., *UNIX Implementation*, UNIX Programmer's Manual, 4.3BSD, Programmer's Supplementary Documents Volume 2, April, 1986. Originally published in the Version 7 UPM, 1977.

Index

Colophon

Our look is the result of reader comments, our own experimentation, and distribution channels.

Distinctive covers complement our distinctive approach to UNIX documentation, breathing personality and life into potentially dry subjects. UNIX and its attendant programs can be unruly beasts. Nutshell Handbooks help you tame them.

The animal featured on the cover of *Using C on the UNIX System* is a lion, a large, carnivorous cat inhabiting western India and Africa south of the Sahara. The most sociable of cats, lions live in prides consisting of one to four males and a collection of up to thirty females and cubs. However, the members of a pride are seldom all together at one time, instead moving about their territory as individuals or small groups. A pride's territory may be anywhere from 15 to 150 square miles, depending on the abundance of food, and is marked by scent and roaring.

Lions eat both fresh kill and carrion—dead animals or the kill of other animals. When they do kill, they show a preference for large prey such as zebra or wildebeest which will feed the entire pride. Females do the majority of the hunting, frequently working cooperatively to encircle or bring down large game. During the hunt, lions are careful to move under cover of darkness or foliage, but tend to disregard the wind direction and thus frequently give themselves away.

Edie Freedman designed this cover and the entire UNIX bestiary that appears on other Nutshell Handbooks. The beasts themselves are adapted from 19th-century engravings from the Dover Pictorial Archive.

The text of this book is set in Times Roman; headings are Helvetica; examples are Courier. Text was prepared using SoftQuad's *sqtroff* text formatter. Printing is done on an Apple LaserWriter.

Books That Help People Get More Out of Computers

If you want more information about our books, or want to know where to buy them, we're happy to send it.

❑ Send me a free catalog of titles.

❑ What bookstores in my area carry your books (U.S. and Canada only)?

❑ Where can I buy your books outside the U.S. and Canada?

❑ Send me information about consulting services for documentation or programming.

Name _____

Address _____

_____

City _____

State, ZIP _____

Country _____

NAME _____

COMPANY _____

ADDRESS _____

CITY _____ STATE _____ ZIP _____

BUSINESS REPLY MAIL

FIRST CLASS MAIL PERMIT NO. 80 SEBASTOPOL, CA

POSTAGE WILL BE PAID BY ADDRESSEE

O'Reilly & Associates, Inc.

103 Morris Street Suite A
Sebastopol CA 95472-9902

‖‖‖‖‖‖‖‖‖‖‖‖‖‖‖‖‖‖‖‖‖‖‖‖‖‖‖‖‖